Letters from Clara

Letters from Clara

～

One Intrepid Woman's Travels
on the Eve of War, 1936–1939

Janet Newman

WISCONSIN HISTORICAL SOCIETY PRESS

Published by the Wisconsin Historical Society Press
Publishers since 1855

The Wisconsin Historical Society helps people connect to the past by collecting, preserving, and sharing stories. Founded in 1846, the Society is one of the nation's finest historical institutions.

Join the Wisconsin Historical Society: wisconsinhistory.org/membership

Front and back cover images courtesy of Wausua YWCA Archives; front cover image donated to the YWCA by Gordon Hackbarth

Printed in Canada
Cover designed by Steve Biel
Typesetting by Sara DeHaan

26 25 24 23 22   1 2 3 4 5

Library of Congress Cataloging-in-Publication Data

Names: Newman, Janet, 1952– author.
Title: Letters from Clara : one intrepid woman's travels on the eve of war, 1936–1939 / Janet Newman.
Description: [Madison, Wisconsin] : Wisconsin Historical Society Press, [2022]
Identifiers: LCCN 2021046164 (print) | LCCN 2021046165 (ebook) | ISBN 9780870209871 (trade paperback) | ISBN 9780870209888 (ebook)
Subjects: LCSH: Pagel, Clara, 1896–1955—Travel. | Pagel, Clara, 1896–1955—Correspondence. | Women travelers—United States—Biography. | Young Women's Christian associations—Biography. | Voyages around the world.
Classification: LCC G440.P146 N48 2022 (print) | LCC G440.P146 (ebook) | DDC 910.4/1092 [B]—dc23/eng/20220128
LC record available at https://lccn.loc.gov/2021046164
LC ebook record available at https://lccn.loc.gov/2021046165

♾ The paper used in this publication meets the minimum requirements of the American National Standard for Information Sciences—Permanence of Paper for Printed Library Materials, ANSI Z39.48-1992.

For women whose stories are unfinished,
untold, or unacknowledged

Contents

Preface

The scent of gardenia wafts through memories of my first days on the job as executive director of the Wausau YWCA in 1993. I had been welcomed with a gardenia corsage and a reception at the organization's neoclassical building on the corner of Fifth and Grant in the city's downtown. The rich history of the organization and the enduring elegance of the building enveloped me: the echoes of determined footsteps on the terrazzo floor, the murmurings of women and girls gathered around the four fireplaces, the rustling of period costumes in the antique study club's clothing collection at the top of the open staircase, the creaking of the ladderback chairs positioned on either side of a gateleg table in my office. It all spoke to me. A portrait of Alma Blandin, the first executive director, hung in my office next to a bay window overlooking the courtyard. I began to imagine all those who had entered the building through the heavy red door over the years since 1920. When I discovered Clara Pagel, all those imaginings of yesteryear sprang to life.

The intoxicating fragrance of the flowers had not yet faded days later when I dived into the filing cabinet in my office. Hiding among the financial records, annual reports, personnel files, and membership records was a folder labeled "Letters from Clara." It didn't seem to belong with the rest, so I set it on my desk, where it was soon buried under the pressing issues of fundraising, refurbishing, and programming. Then one Friday afternoon, in an ambitious attempt to clear my desk, I took the folder home and the next morning took it along as we left on a family road trip. My husband drove and I turned my attention to the folder. Typed on the top of the first page was "Hong Kong, November 9, 1936." Flipping to the end of the letter, I found the closing: "Love to you all, Clara." I began to read aloud. As the miles sped by, I was increasingly intrigued by the colorful descriptions and insights into humanity. My husband was fascinated by the historic context. The last letter was written from a ship, dated July 22, 1939, with the inside address "Leaving Dar-es-Salam" (Tanzania). I had no idea whether Clara was a real person or the letters were a literary device. The overriding mystery was why the file folder was at the YWCA.

Unlocking the mystery has been a thrilling adventure, one that involved some sleuthing. With the help of Mary Jane Hettinga, executive director of the Marathon County Historical Society at the time, I found Clara Pagel's date of death, which led to cranking through microfilm in the Marathon County Public Library, searching for her obituary and any other mention of her in the *Wausau Daily Record-Herald*. From there, I began to unspool information from people's musty minds and attics. Scouring the YWCA's own dusty archives in preparation for the seventy-fifth anniversary celebration of the organization, former YWCA staff member Ellen Hartwig and I found photographs of Clara. Through interviews with three people who knew Clara and through various newspaper clippings and other items in the YWCA archives, one of which was an interview with this remarkable woman, I pieced together a picture of Clara's life. But it was the one hundred pages of letters she sent to friends and the YWCA Wausau's Blue Triangle Club that held the most promise of revealing who Clara Pagel was and why she set off alone on a trip around the world in 1936. She had just turned forty, and the world was on the precipice of war.

A letter is a much richer form of communication than an email, text message, or even a phone conversation, and it can still create the same sense of immediacy. By taking the time to compose a letter, distractions give way to reflection and attention to detail. While the audible notification of an incoming email or text message sometimes quickens a heart, it is much less satisfying than the anticipation of retrieving a letter from a mailbox, opening it with a weighty letter opener, unfolding it, and reading it. Unlike a hurried text, email, or phone call, a letter reveals details about the writer's interests, concerns, and surroundings. A letter is also enduring. It can be reread, tucked away for safekeeping, and taken out again and again to enjoy. Years after both the recipient and the writer are gone, someone may find the letter and delight in it all over again. Such was the case with these letters from Clara. If Clara Pagel hadn't been a letter writer, her story would have been lost.

I'm old enough to have been a letter writer myself. When I went to Cambridge, England, as a student teacher in my final year of undergraduate study, I immediately began to record my impressions in daily letters written on blue foldable onionskin airmail stationery. Most often, I was writing to the man I married three years later. I grew increasingly anxious as days and weeks went by without receiving a single letter in reply, until the day I returned to my apartment to find a month's worth of letters strewn all over the floor below the mail slot. I kept that day's letters and those that faithfully followed. Those long-awaited letters have been treasured and now give our daughter a glimpse into her parents' dreams, worries, and joys.

Clara, too, would have eagerly awaited letters from home. When she was in Shanghai, mail between the United States and China was carried via the fastest ocean liner of the day, the *Empress of Japan*. It ordinarily took a month or more, but for three months in late 1936 and early 1937, the seamen's strike on the Pacific Coast of the United States halted mail delivery to China entirely. When Clara was in Manila, it took only a week to receive mail. The *China Clipper*, the first flying boat built for Pan

American Airways, initiated commercial transpacific airmail service between San Francisco and Manila in late 1935. (Movies from the United States also arrived via the *China Clipper*, so when Clara was in Manila, she was seeing American movies at the same time as her friends back in Wausau.) When Clara was on the move, she would receive mail at an American Express office or through the Thomas Cook & Son travel agency. Clara sent and received a few cablegrams to mark special occasions.

Not all letters sent by Clara reached their destination. In addition to the straightforward reasons that mail goes astray, censorship and confiscation became a concern, especially in Italy in 1939. Even earlier in her journey, though, Japan's occupation of China led to correspondence obstacles. By that time, Clara was in Manila, but she was able to deliver letters to China via an Anglican mission and a business firm. On at least one occasion, she was able to receive a smuggled letter via a Philippine shopkeeper who went to Beijing to make business purchases.

The letters I first discovered had been retyped, which made me wonder initially if they were a literary vehicle from a fictional Clara. I came to understand that at the time, Clara's letters were being compiled at the YWCA and read aloud during meetings of the Blue Triangle Club. They were retyped so that the original letter could be returned to the recipient. The retyping led to errors, which caused me much consternation. For example, the year might be mistyped, or an unfamiliar word might be retyped as a word with an entirely different meaning. Some of the letters had evidently been retyped yet again in more recent years, perhaps for inclusion in a newsletter, so some words were typed with their current spelling rather than the original (*rickshaw vs. ricksha* is one example). Clara was very precise about spelling. In one letter, she explained that both "Hong Kong" and "Hongkong" are correct. She frequently referred to variations when names were romanized. I have no confidence that the person doing the retyping was as precise. Clara's letter-writing conventions also were not replicated. I know that because I eventually obtained a few originals of letters Clara had sent to the family with whom she lived just prior to her departure for Asia. Clara took a lot of care with her salutations. Even when she used a term of endearment, she punctuated the salutation with a colon. Many of the retyped letters do not even identify to whom the letter was addressed. Similarly, her closings were sometimes colorfully written but were often omitted in the retyped letters. Whenever possible, I reverted to spellings and conventions that most likely reflect the original.

The stationery on which the original letters were typed or handwritten also contributes to Clara's story. One letter from Manila was typed on letterhead from the American Trade Commissioner, another was typed on hotel stationery. Most of the letters from China were printed on onionskin embellished with what appear to be hand-painted butterflies and flowers. Those letters were sent in matching envelopes. A few of the letters were handwritten and even included Clara's sketches. Her handwriting is careful—but not cramped—with an occasional flourish. That's an apt description of her personality, too.

It's important to note that the letters, presented just as they were written in the 1930s, contain some language choices and perspectives that are offensive today. Clara was aware of her limited world view and embarked on these travels precisely because she wanted to increase her understanding. Open to reconsidering her prejudices and critical judgments, she loved learning about cultures and traditions, and the letters convey a growing sensitivity to and appreciation of differences. Even when she uses terms now considered derogatory, it's clear that she sees the humanity in the people she encounters and delights in those interactions. I find it heartening that her curiosity about varied cultural, sociological, and economic influences allowed her to move beyond initial impressions and discard certain assumptions.

The names of cities and countries are included as Clara referred to them at the time. Beijing in Clara's day was called Peiping (Peking being the romanized version of the name). Most other cities in China are referred to by their romanized versions in the letters. Similarly, the names of African towns in what was then Italian Somaliland are Italianized. Some countries Clara visited have been re-named since the 1930s—for example, Burma is now Myanmar, and Ceylon is now Sri Lanka. Also, the borders of some nations have changed—some were undergoing change even as Clara was writing these letters.

Twenty-five years after first discovering the letters, I resolved to carry out Clara's wishes to have them bound. The letters themselves, along with information about her life before and after her three-year adventure, relate the story of a fascinating woman. I returned to the YWCA to retrieve pictures, letters, and the 1928 Remington portable typewriter that accompanied Clara on her trip around the world. I had placed these items in the safe at the YWCA when I left my position there in 1999. Sometime during the intervening years, the safe fell out of use and the combination was forgotten, so I contacted Paul Clarke, criminal justice faculty member at Northcentral Technical College and part-time deputy in the Marathon County Sheriff's Department, asking if he could direct me to a safecracker. On a dark and cold night in March 2019, Paul and his friend John Rupple literally cracked open the safe, utilizing a grinder, sledgehammer, pry bar, chisel, and mallet. I was on St. Croix in the US Virgin Islands at the time, but I shared in the excitement via Facetime and texts.

All these years after first opening a file folder, through several decades of advances in the ability to access information, I am still inspired by the story of a woman from yesteryear who set her sights on the wider world.

1

A Journey's Beginnings

July 5, 1936. It was on this day that Clara Pagel left Wausau, Wisconsin, for what she intended to be a two-year trip around the world. Accompanying her was Erna Flatter, a missionary from Wausau who was returning to China. I feel certain that Clara would have taken in a fireworks display the evening before her departure. The effervescence of the fireworks would have reflected her own feelings of bubbling excitement about finally being free to pursue a dream she'd kept bottled up for a very long time. She might have said she felt "thrilled to her toes" for both her country's independence and her own. But the next morning, she no doubt felt more somber, almost nostalgic. Having settled her mother's estate, she would have felt unmoored—which she was, in more ways than one. Clara was alone in the world with no family and was about to embark by ship on her longed-for trip around the world.

On July 9, she boarded the passenger ship *Hansa* in the port of New York. As she set off for Germany, Clara might have thought of her mother, Johanna Kramer. When Johanna left Germany in 1871, she could not afford a steamship ticket, so her trip was aboard a sailboat. Just twenty years old, she was seasick for weeks and prayed to reach Wausau safely, where her older sister lived. How Clara wished her mother had reached a place of safety and calm when she arrived and began working as a housekeeper for Ernest Pagel, a widowed saloon keeper.

BECOMING CLARA

In 1889, Johanna married Ernest Pagel. She gave birth to Arthur in 1892, and four years later, at the age of forty-five, she had Clara. When Clara was fifteen, her father died; she was sixteen when her brother, Arthur, died from a self-inflicted gunshot wound to the head. In a front-page news item in the *Stevens Point Daily Journal*, Arthur was described by Johanna as ambitious to a fault, exhausting himself with studying at night and working during the day. According to the article, he had been diagnosed with "congestion of the liver and stomach" and had been hallucinating from a "brain fever."[1] Clara's mother, arguing that Arthur did not intend to kill himself, sued the life insurance company, which had denied the claim, maintaining that the death was by suicide. The case went to a jury trial, and Clara's mother prevailed. The verdict was appealed to the Wisconsin Supreme Court, which upheld the lower court's decision. Johanna's tough-minded determination in defending her son and battling the insurance company would certainly have had an impact on her teenage daughter.

Two deaths in consecutive years was a lot of grief to endure, but the Pagel home had never been a happy one. According to an interview with Clara conducted in 1928 as part of a national YWCA on-site visit to determine the extent to which the Wausau YWCA was meeting its mission, Clara's father had exerted control over everyone's activities. Clara and her mother were not allowed to attend church because the minister had criticized Ernest from the pulpit for his abusive treatment of his first wife. When Clara

---

1. "Suicide at Wausau; Ill Health and Overwork Given as Cause," *Stevens Point Daily Journal*, August 20, 1912.

graduated from high school in 1914, as much as she longed to leave for college, she remained at home to care for her mother. She did so until her mother, who had become paralyzed, died in 1932.

Throughout her life, Clara embodied the motto chosen by her Wausau High School graduating class: "We are conquered by no adversities." At their five-year reunion, on Armistice Day, a newspaper article noted that "the class graduated in one of the most turbulent years of the world's history, 1914 being marked by the great cataclysm of the world's war."[2] The journey Clara took twenty years later occurred as the next cataclysmic world war began to unfold.

After her father died, Clara became active in the church and Bible study. In the interview with national YWCA staff, she said she was taught to believe the Bible "from cover to cover, every word," but that the executive director of the YWCA truly opened the Bible for her. She said, "At first I had to argue for the minister, and he was terribly worried about me and then I discovered it was my job to think for myself but not necessarily to try to change everybody's way of thinking."[3] She also met Erna (Ernie) Flatter, who became a missionary to China. This friendship expanded Clara's horizons. Clara's independence of mind and resistance to religious indoctrination disqualified her for missionary work, but she thought that immersing herself in a part of the world so far from the familiar would be "terribly interesting," a phrase she used repeatedly in her letters.

The Wausau YWCA was established in 1920. Clara's mother thought it was a safe place for her daughter to go in the evenings. The role the YWCA played in enlarging Clara's circumscribed life cannot be overstated. It promoted her development as a person

---

2. "'14 Class Reunion Big Success," *Wausau Daily Record-Herald*, June 30, 1919.
3. From "Record of Interview," appendix to a 1928 report by the YWCA of the USA, Wausau YWCA archive.

who lived up to her potential, and it enabled her to undertake a journey of discovery around the world. In Clara's own words, "Y.W.C.A. has just done everything for me. All my dearest friends, and I have so many, I found there."[4]

CLARA AND THE YWCA

The Young Women's Christian Association is the oldest and largest multicultural women's organization in the world. Today, it has members in 122 countries. Founded in 1855 in London, the first YWCAs in the United States were in New York City and Boston, where women's residences were opened in 1858. In 1894, YWCA Traveler's Aid was established, serving to protect women traveling in steerage from violent crimes. In 1909, the YWCA began to offer bilingual instruction for immigrant women, and in 1919, it convened the first International Conference of Women Physicians with representation from thirty-two countries. It is against this backdrop of women helping one another that Clara Pagel, at the age of twenty-four, joined the YWCA of Wausau when its doors opened. There she found opportunities to satisfy her curiosity and creativity, opportunities to quench her thirst for friendship and fulfillment, and opportunities for intellectual stimulation and leadership development.

The Wausau newspaper reported in 1921 that Clara addressed the Rotary Club in an appeal for financial support of the YWCA. In a foreshadowing of how Clara herself benefited from the YWCAs in various parts of the world, the story reads, "Miss Clara H. Pagel gave a very clear and strong appeal for support of the Young Women's Christian Association, telling of the direct benefits derived by girls of the city and country, and of the help the association is to rich and poor; to the young girls especially

---

4. "Record of Interview."

when away from home in a strange city. Her talk was effective and finely made."[5] Clara, an early and dedicated fundraiser for the YWCA, made the same appeal to the Kiwanis.

Clara enjoyed the YWCA lectures and discussions, studying stars and trees and early Wisconsin history—so many things that almost made up for not having gone to college. She sang in the YWCA choir, belonged to the Literary Guild and Book of the Month Club, attended concerts, and performed in plays. She once performed the role of St. George in a mummer's play staged for a Twelfth Night party. She not only had the height to play St. George, she had assumed a dragon slayer's disposition.

Alma Blandin, Wausau YWCA executive director, fostered Clara's confidence and ambition. She recruited Clara for the board of directors and encouraged her as she carried out leadership positions. Clara served on the board from 1922 to 1925 and again from 1930 to 1933. The 1930–33 Official Ballot for Election to the Board of Directors for the Wausau Young Women's Christian Association describes Clara, one of thirteen people running for nine spots, as "Business girl, charter member Blue Triangle Club, First Reformed church, member of Board of Directors one term, served as Secretary, member of Young Women's Council and Blue Triangle committees, frequently chairman of short term club projects, auditor of Building campaign and all Finance campaigns."[6] Anyone unmarried was identified as a "business girl," whereas a married candidate was identified as a "home woman." The board had twenty-seven members. After the nine members whose terms were expiring were not counted, it was noted on the ballot that sixteen of the remaining eighteen were home women.

5. "Miss Clara H. Pagel Asks Rotary Help for Young Women's Christian Association," *Wausau Daily Record-Herald*, December 6, 1921.
6. Official Ballot for Election to Board of Directors Young Women's Christian Association Wausau, Wisconsin Term 1930–1933 "Who's Who" on the Ballot, Wausau YWCA archive.

So business girls were in the minority. Clara truly was a business girl, and not just because she was unmarried. Having completed coursework at the business school in Wausau, she became executive secretary to Guy Gooding, president of the Wisconsin Box Company, in 1924.

The Blue Triangle Club, comprising exclusively business girls, was named for the blue triangle logo, which identified YWCAs throughout the world. As indicated on the ballot, Clara was involved in establishing that club, which connected her with other career-minded women. The Blue Triangle Club was a tight-knit group of dynamic women. They discussed current issues, such as foreign policy and economic policy. One year, they studied the munitions industry. The Blue Triangle Club threw a send-off party for Clara the month before she left on her worldwide tour. Most of the letters Clara wrote on that trip were addressed to members of the Blue Triangle Club, either individually or collectively; reading the letters aloud became a regular agenda item between 1936 and 1939. In one such letter, Clara harked back to a speaker who years before, in addressing the group, had asked if they would understand a reference to the Plankinton Arcade, a building in Milwaukee, two hundred miles away. Clara took umbrage at the speaker's assumption that their horizons were limited to communities adjoining Wausau, saying, "Guess she thought Brokaw and Rothschild were our horizons."[7] World Fellowship Day was an important one in the YWCA calendar. A newspaper article, in describing a Blue Triangle banquet held on that day, noted that Clara, the Blue Triangle Club's "geographer," placed a blue triangle on a world map as greetings from each location were read, showing that the YWCA "literally extends 'round the

---

7. Letter from Clara to Irma Gebhard, June 25, 1939.

world.'"[8] It is easy to imagine that placing those blue triangles on the world map sparked Clara's desire to visit them one day.

Alma Blandin not only helped Clara expand her horizons— she also helped Clara see that, despite lacking adequate financial resources, her dream of traveling around the world was possible. Alma explained that her friend from college, Lelia Hinkley, who was working as an overseas secretary for the YWCA in China, could help Clara find a job.

Between 1895 and 1970, more than eight hundred professional staff of the YWCA of the USA served in a variety of capacities in more than thirty countries. They were referred to as "secretaries," which, at the time, was the title for professionals employed by the YWCA. They worked as teachers, social workers, public health experts, hostel managers, and agricultural advisors in cooperation with the local YWCAs. The heyday of the YWCA's international work occurred in Asia and Europe from 1915 through the end of World War II.

Years later, in 1957, Elizabeth Johns, who served as a YWCA of the USA secretary to Burma and Ceylon,[9] explained that the benefits did not flow in just one direction:

> It is no sacrifice to America to have sent these hundreds
> of young women to serve. They come back and interpret;
> they come back and work in our Associations with enlarged
> perspectives, new vision and ideas. They help us to conquer
> our provincial attitudes, our complacency, and help us to
> think as world citizens. Those who "love by serving one
> another" grow in understanding of the deeper meaning of our
> purpose and our task. This is no sacrifice but a rare privilege,

---

8. "Business Girls Hold Nationwide Banquet at YWCA," *Wausau Daily Record-Herald*, March 25, 1931.
9. Burma is now Myanmar and Ceylon is now Sri Lanka.

for which all of us in the sending Associations must give
thanks.[10]

It was a rare privilege for Clara to access this network of
women and derive the benefits Johns described.

At the time of Clara's trip, there was a close association between missionaries and YWCA overseas secretaries. Missionary
societies initially sent out only married couples and a few single
men, with wives serving as unpaid assistants. Women at the time
were not ordained, and the prevailing attitude was that unmarried
women should not live unprotected and alone in a foreign country. However, in China, the cultural norms were such that male
missionaries could not interact with Chinese women, so by 1844,
the first unmarried female missionary went to China to open a
school for girls. One way in which the work of missionaries and
the YWCA overlapped in China was in their creation of schools
for women. Another way was in their opposition to foot binding.
Clara had both missionary and YWCA connections in China, so
that is where she first paused in her journey.

STAYING CONNECTED

It took Clara nearly four years to settle her mother's estate. For
the most part, it probably felt like an unburdening. But when it
came to her own possessions, I imagine that Clara became sentimental—especially about selling her Oldsmobile. After all, when
she bought it in the early 1930s, it gave her a taste of travel beyond
the confines of Wausau. Her first adventure in the Olds involved
setting out for the Kentucky Derby with a load of Blue Trianglers,

---

10. Nancy Boyd, *Emissaries: The Overseas Work of the American YWCA
1895–1970* (New York: Woman's Press, 1986), 257.

after just one driving lesson from the salesman. This escapade was relayed to me by Phillip "Bud" Morgan, the nephew of Clara's dearest friend, Irma Gebhard. Irma and Clara were neighbors and were both members of the Blue Triangle Club. Irma's sister, Lydia, was married to Roy Morgan. During the time between the sale of her mother's home and her departure for her trip around the world, Clara lived with the Morgan family. The Morgans treated Clara as one of their own, and Clara felt at home with them.

At the time when Clara embarked on her journey, the Morgans' son was ten years old. When I met Bud, fifty-seven years after Clara returned from her trip, he gave me letters from Clara, some of them handwritten. They had been stored in his parents' attic, along with the typewriter that accompanied Clara on her trip—a 1928 portable Remington, ingeniously designed with folding typebars. The typewriter case is plastered with baggage claims, including one from Port Said, Egypt, and hotel stickers, including one from Athens. Next to its lock is printed

C. H. Pagel
Wausau–Wisconsin
U.S.A.

My appreciation for Clara's qualities was enhanced when I met Bud, who called her a "woman of derring-do." Not only was he someone who knew Clara personally, but he had carried on a correspondence with her while she was on her trip, even though he was an elementary-school-age boy at the time. Some of the letters in the attic had been addressed to him, and they revealed aspects of Clara's life and personality I would otherwise not have discovered. In one of the letters, Clara tells Bud's mother, Lydia, that she's pasting his letters into her scrapbook and is carrying his picture in her purse, together with a picture of his Aunt Irma, saying, "It's such a comfortable feeling to know they are there."[11] It is clear that this family meant a lot to Clara, who often described herself as being without a family.

Based on Clara's responses to Bud's letters, it is obvious that he sent her jokes and had asked her if she had ever ridden a bicycle. In turn, she told him that she did not like the Mae West film *Go West, Young Man* and that she saw a film that was supposedly set in a Wisconsin lumber camp and was not at all accurate. She told him that she missed her Victrola. The exchanges show a mutual affection and a great deal of familiarity with one another's interests and activities.

Clara also sent gifts to Bud and carefully considered the condition in which they might arrive. In a letter to his mother, Clara says,

> This knife is from Hangchow,[12] a place noted for its cutlery.
> . . . I wish, before you give the knife to [him], you would
> look to see if the steel blade has any rust on it. China is an
> extremely damp country and things rust quickly, so the
> knife may become somewhat rusted in transit. . . . And if
> someone opens a box only to find a rusted something inside,
> I think it takes away some of the pleasure of receiving it,
> so I'd appreciate your scouring it if some rust should have
> accumulated. Thanks.

Clara lamented that there were some things from China she could not send because of shipping constraints.

> Oh, the kites out here, Lyd! This evening I stood outside
> and saw a large fluttering butterfly in one direction, a huge

---

11. Letter from Clara to Lydia Morgan, January 8, 1936.
12. Sometimes spelled Hankow, now known as Hangzhou.

dragonfly in another, and a lovely sort of "double Junebug" way up high. Oh, they are <u>so</u> pretty! I want to send home a box full, but I don't know how to do it. They are made of bamboo in such a way that I can't send them in pieces. . . .

I saw a man on the street last week carrying around some beautiful little models of battleships; I did so want to send one home to [him], but I knew it would never reach Wausau in any reasonable condition since they are so fragile.

Bud was by no means the only person who received gifts from Clara. She was a thoughtful and prolific gift-giver. Handkerchiefs were frequently inserted with her letters from China. In one such letter, Clara explains that "China is noted for handkerchiefs, at least I know her exports of handkerchiefs have a place in customs statistical reports."[13]

When Clara's friend Arletta Petzold got married in October 1937, the wedding notice carried in the Wausau newspaper said the bride "had the distinction of wearing a gown of brocaded satin sent her from China by Clara Pagel."[14] It also mentioned that the couple had received a cable from Clara. I was fortunate to meet Arletta's husband, Gordon Hackbarth, nearly sixty years later. Gordon had read the October 7, 1995, *Wausau Daily Herald* front-page article about my discovery of Clara's letters and invited me to visit him at the home of his daughter in Stewartville, Minnesota. During the Saturday afternoon I spent with him, he regaled me with stories about the legendary Clara, gave me a picture of Clara atop a camel in front of the pyramids, and told me about the friendship between Clara and Emmett Kelly, the man who performed as the first-ever sad-faced clown, dubbed Weary Willy. Clara, who drove 279 miles to Chicago to have lunch with

---

13. Letter from Clara to Lydia Morgan, February 18, 1937.
14. "News of Society," *Wausau Daily Record-Herald*, October 21, 1937.

Mr. Kelly, inspired Arletta to collect clowns.[15] Clara had asked
Arletta to accompany her on the trip around the world, but Arletta declined because she had just gotten engaged. It's touching
to know that Clara sent Arletta fabric from China for her wedding
dress. It was a gesture Gordon never forgot.

Clara often sent items to the Blue Triangle Club for use as
party favors or table decorations for their dinners. Newspaper
items describing those events frequently mentioned that fact and
that letters from Clara were read aloud at the event. Even though
Clara was a lone traveler, she took her many friends along on a
trip around the world through her letters and gifts.

SETTING OFF

After resigning from her job, after the farewells, after promises to
write, Clara was finally on her way with a typewriter to record all
her impressions. She would have set off with thanks to her mother
and the inheritance that launched her. The dollar amount would
not get her far, but her mother's spirit-crushing life spurred Clara
to live her own life with purpose. Clara may have been influenced
by Eleanor Roosevelt to venture off, alone, to who knows where.
Roosevelt is often quoted as saying, "The purpose of life, after all,
is to live it, to taste experience to the utmost, to reach out eagerly
and without fear for newer and richer experience."

Clara and Erna's first stop was Germany, where Clara searched
for her aunts. According to Olga Block, Clara's second cousin,
correspondence with the aunts had stopped after World War I.
According to another second cousin, Will Kalinke, Clara hoped

---

15. In 1934, there were twenty-three Wisconsin members of the Circus Fans
    Association of America, only three of whom were women. Clara was one
    of them, along with Mrs. Al Ringling. "Circus Fans Meet Beneath Big
    Top for Madison Show; New Association Conducts Its Annual Session
    at Capital City," *Green Bay Press-Gazette*, August 6, 1934.

to determine whether her aunts had emigrated to Argentina. After they visited Erna's aunt in a German village, Erna continued on to China. Unable to locate her aunts, Clara left Germany and traveled for a few months wherever her curiosity took her.

Between July 1936 and the first letter I found, which was dated November 1936, Clara visited Ceylon, India, Burma, Indo-China, Thailand, Malaya, Singapore, Indonesia, and the Philippines. She visited YWCAs in many of these countries and toured alone until she arrived in China. That is where, using both missionary and YWCA connections, she began to settle in. The letters she sent from China begin to paint a picture of a spirited, curious, open-minded woman in the mid-1930s—one who, in the words of Secretary to Burma and Ceylon Elizabeth Johns, was seeking an enlarged perspective and new vision and ideas; seeking to conquer her provincial attitude and complacency; seeking to think as a world citizen. What a tumultuous time it proved to be!

2

Arrival in China

The first letter I found in the file folder was no doubt addressed to Clara's dearest friend, Irma Gebhard, though no name is mentioned. No one else would have received the "darling" salutation. Irma would have, in turn, shared it with others at a meeting of the Blue Triangle Club. In this first letter, we are introduced to Clara's rich descriptions, strong opinions, colorful way of expressing herself, fascination with the antics of children, sense of humor, sarcasm, and recollections of home.

> Hong Kong
> November 9, 1936
> Darling:
> As per usual, I'm crazy about Hong Kong! It's very clean—
> exceptionally so. Of course, you know it's not exactly
> Chinese. England has a "lease" on it and naturally the English
> influence is in the air and you meet the English in every place
> of importance. I used to get impatient about England taking
> in as much territory all over the world, but it really is very
> comfortable, after traveling in a country like Java and trying
> to deal with the Dutch, to again land in a country where you
> run into the English language all along the street. . . .
> Hong Kong is very, very large. Part of it is on an island.

A part, called Kowloon, is on the mainland. I rode down the main street of the latter and at one place I felt as though I were on Michigan Blvd. The street was so clean it simply shone. However, I understand that a few blocks over, there is filth plus. But then, we have Maxwell Street, too.[1] On the island, the city is partly built on a hill. It rises up back of the town high, I think, like Rib Hill.[2] Houses are built all over it—on the awfullest crags. I don't understand why some of them don't fall off. A cable car goes up at one point, and in one place it seems to actually stand on end. You'd love that ride, and the one in rickshas going around the peak at the top. (I thought of you.)

But at night when the entire town is lit up! It is hard to tell where the lights on the hill end and the stars begin. The sight is so dazzling, so beautiful, that I almost wanted to weep! With the many colored neon lights on the buildings toward the bottom, the whole town looks like a mammoth Christmas tree. I went over to Kowloon by ferry Sunday night, and on the way back sat and gazed and gazed—I couldn't get my fill. Last night again I watched the lights until they dimmed in the distance.

Sunday night I went over to Kowloon to attend a service in a mission where my cabinmate's father spoke. It is located among the poor Chinese. It was very funny to me. Beside me was an old woman. She had her bare feet perched up on the bench in front of her, and a baby sitting on that bench kept playing with her toes! Pretty soon the old woman realized what was going on, and kept pulling away, but the baby was undaunted.

Late afternoon—on train back to Hong Kong
Of all the dirty, smelly, unpleasant, unsightly, un-everything

---

1. Michigan Avenue and Maxwell Street are located in Chicago.
2. Now known as Rib Mountain.

in the dictionary, Canton[3] is it! I wouldn't commit suicide
in this city. Oh, it is <u>awful</u>. We rode on a sight-seeing tour all
morning—miles out to the university, and miles through the
city streets, and there isn't a pleasant thing to look back to.
Only one thing I recall with any enthusiasm whatever was a
chrysanthemum exhibit in a park. (And when I say "park,"
eliminate the thought of grass.) What very little there is in
and around the city is brown and dusty and coarse. They
grow the chrysanthemums in pots, and when they blossom,
bamboo is stuck in to hold the stems in a certain direction,
and they are arranged so they form a regular dome—very
queer. Almost every plant was arranged that way. Flowers not
large, but 100s in a single plant.

India may be dirty, but I'll choose it any day in preference
to Canton. I believe this is the first time since leaving home
that I've said bad things about any place. We walked down
some streets to see temples or pagodas, etc., that were
narrower than our alleys—patch of cement here; large flat
stones there; hard sand farther on; mud; stinking food stalls;
pigs, dogs, geese, horrible! Hong Kong will look like Paradise
to me in three hours. I want to jump into a bathtub and wash
all my clothes, certainly scrubbing my shoes. I feel as though
the corners of my mouth are definitely turned down in a
permanent expression of repugnance and disgust.

Even though missionaries provided some of the linkages that
allowed Clara to travel, it wasn't long before she began to wonder
whether missionaries were doing a disservice. She may have read
Pearl Buck's twin biographies of Buck's parents, which advanced

---

3. Guangzhou.

the notion that foreign missions were a form of imperialism.[4]
Whether or not she had, the opportunity to observe missionary
work for herself and discuss it with others stimulated her thinking.

> Hong Kong
> November 16, 1936
> People out here and all through the Orient from India on
> haven't many nice things to say about missionaries. In India
> and along down the Malays they who talked about missions
> would compliment the medical work, praise it highly, but not
> the evangelistic or educational. I've heard so many people
> say most unkind things about them. . . . It's funny, but one
> of the main objections seems to be, especially in Bali, that
> the missionaries dress the natives instead of letting them go
> nude, as they have been going for hundreds of years. Another
> objection is that missionaries are too prim and proper.

Clara also experienced the "educational" value of lighthearted
pursuits. The letter continues:

> I'm beginning to get quite educated on drinks. I've met and
> struck up a standing friendship with the "gimlet"—even
> know how to make it. The Manhattan Cocktail is no longer a
> stranger; neither is the silver gin fizz. The Honolulu Cocktail
> is delicious, although not yet on familiar terms with it. I had
> something all mixed up in Bangkok that made me take only
> two sips—some egg concoction.
>   Did I say I went on this trip for purely educational
> purposes? I'm getting the education all right—but in far

---

4. Pearl S. Buck, *The Exile: Portrait of an American Mother* (New York: John
   Day, 1936) and *Fighting Angel: Portrait of a Soul* (New York: Reynal &
   Hitchcock, 1936).

different lines than I ever expected to. Travel is broadening;
I prefer to use the word "opening." It takes the Orient to
knock the props out from under. If only I could stick around
a year or two. I'm so afraid of snapping back before my mind
stretches enough to make it permanent.

By December 1936, Clara connected with Lelia Hinkley, a
YWCA international secretary in Shanghai who had gone through
training with Alma Blandin. Clara lived temporarily with Lelia,
working for the YWCA while seeking more steady employment.
Clara was surprised that her idea of working her way around the
world was not unique, saying if she had known how hard it was
going to be to "land an office job in Shanghai," she would never
have had the courage to attempt it. One of Clara's first small-world
encounters was with another woman seeking employment who
had worked in New York City for the brokerage that handled
Eastern business for Wisconsin Box, the company for which Clara
had worked in Wausau.

The first letter from Shanghai begins with a description of
shopping. Clara was always on the lookout for gifts to send home,
but in this letter, she writes about her weakness for lingerie and
coats.

Shanghai, China
November 24, 1936
I saw some of the most beautiful underwear today! Oh, it
was exquisite! I get into these shops and forget all about
there being something worthwhile seeing outside of them.
Embroideries! Jewelry! Undies!!! And oh, one Mandarin
coat—$155! I fell for an embroidered cape in Hong Kong.
It is a queerly-fashioned affair—entirely covered with
embroidered, eyeletted, punch-worked, French-knotted
flowers, and much be-fringed. I call it my Ming Dynasty cape.
I'm sure there's not another like it in the world. Seriously.

Clara was only a few months into her trip when, in the same letter, she summed up her experience with a sentiment that would be repeated many times throughout the next three years.

> On this trip, I've had some of the grandest, deepest laughs and the loveliest experiences—and I've also hit some of the deepest depths of despair, although when I look back at them, the experiences that caused them were awfully interesting.

～

Clara was attuned to world events. She was receiving Wausau's newspaper, the *Daily Record-Herald*, but through conversations with people from around the world, she was exposed to different perspectives on the news and began to develop skepticism about any news source.

> Shanghai, China
> December 5, 1936
> I was interested in the item in the Record Herald about the silver black fox furs for the king. I could go on for pages as to this king business.[5] You know the English will not discuss it at all. Shortly after "Time" came out with the whole thing, I was discussing it with the girl from Holland, and she said there was absolutely nothing to it. "Why," she said, "the whole English nation knows that the king is homo-sexual and can never marry. Nothing ever appears about it in any of the British territories." When I protested that surely "Time" wouldn't publish anything if there weren't at least a grain of truth in it, the only reply I got was, "Good Lord, you don't believe what the American newspapers print, do you?"

---

5. King Edward VIII (1894–1972) reigned from January 20 to December 10, 1936, when he abdicated in order to marry Wallis Warfield Simpson.

We get an early indication that home is frequently on Clara's mind as the letter continues:

Next day
Walked into the American Chamber of Commerce this p.m.
and on a shelf found a Wausau City Directory! Believe you
me, I grabbed it and just looked and looked. It was of 1931.

I have always thought that if I had a trip around the
world, I should be content the rest of my life. When I listen
around to these secretaries who say: "Last year when we
crossed Siberia." "You know the most thrilling thing I've ever
done was fly from Basra to Persia." "Oh, Jean, I went to the
Grand Hotel for those sandwiches that you introduced me
to in Panama." "No, I didn't come through Austria this time.
I spent 2 months in England instead." "Oh, you should go
down the Yangtze Gorges. I flew over them last year." And
on and on and on, just as if they were saying: "Oh, I stopped
into the Ideal[6] last evening and had one of those parfaits." Or,
"Have you ever been around Rib Hill? You must go with me
some evening."

Although Clara says that she is "crazy about Shanghai," the
most international city she's ever visited, she recognizes that
China is a country of contrasts:

Saturday afternoon I went over to what here is called the
"Chinese City." It is China with a vengeance—absolutely
unspoiled. In the whole afternoon's wanderings, we (Miss
Hinkley and I) met just two other foreigners—two sailors
from some American boat. The streets were terribly narrow,
noisy, cluttered up, pretty dirty, and crooked. I saw a folder

---

6. Ideal Drug Store was located inside the Hotel Wausau.

somewhere some time ago suggesting that visitors be sure
to see the temple and tea house over there, and the pictures
of it looked lovely. The tea house was perhaps at one time
quite nice, but now it looks very much like some old weather-
beaten woodshed, holding together out of pure spite. It is
built on piles in the middle of what politeness calls a lake but
what I would call a quite small pond, about the size of ours
in the fairgrounds. The water is dirty green (like the Chicago
River, only darker) and all around the edge and across to the
tea house is a bridge-like sidewalk. Butting right up against
the edge are the surrounding buildings—all more or less
shacks sadly in need of paint and general tidying up.

    China is funny. You go along the street and see these
straggly shops and dirt all over, and right in the middle of
probably the dirtiest part you will see a gem shop shining out
at you, or a shop with lovely underwear and mandarin coats.

Clara was enchanted by color, sparkle, fabric, and needlework.
But the true beauty of travel for her was that it enhanced her
understanding while challenging her preconceptions. Clara took
the opportunity to accompany YWCA staff to villages outside
of Shanghai. One such excursion, which had a deep impact on
Clara, is described in the following letter. It illustrates her social
consciousness even as she adopts a breezy style.

Shanghai, China
December 13, 1936
Last week one afternoon I went to a small village outside of
Shanghai with the Rural Secretary. The YWCA here has one
regular department devoted to work among the women of
the villages in China. Unfortunately, it began to rain early
in the afternoon and by the time we left at 4:00 it was quite
a downpour. We had to ride in busses that were so jammed

with Chinese peasants that we were almost packed closer
than sardines. And I don't believe there were any springs on
the vehicle, and the gas exhaust came right into the thing, so
between being asphyxiated and compressed, we had a good
time.

It's a little difficult to tell when you have reached a village.
You walk along paths at the edges, or between fields, and
suddenly come to a group of ramshackle, straw-thatched
huts straggling down on each side of a short stretch of hard-
packed ground, or a few huts straggling along a small creek.
Of course nobody owns a horse, or ricksha, and there is no
road. Oh, yes, across a wide creek we did come to a straggling
"Fifth Avenue" which was about the width of our alleys,
paved with jagged stones, and lined on both sides with open
shops of every description—some pretty smelly, and all quite
dirty and dusty and musty and dark and cold and everything
else that made me homesick. But it was all terribly interesting.

One place in particular interested me. There were two
men with a queer contraption that looked for all the world
like a large harp with all but one string gone. They were
fluffing up wool for quilts, and they would hold this thing
over and pull the string so that it would vibrate over the
top of the pile—vibrate enough to give a sort of jump-up
motion and pull up the wool. I stood there a pretty long time
watching them. They pull the string with a wooden mallet-
like affair and it gives the string the queerest sound. We saw
another shop in Shanghai the other evening where they were
doing the same thing and again I stood and gazed.

We went into several houses (altho calling them "houses"
is quite flattering). One place into which we went reminded
me a lot of going into the yard of my aunt out in the town
of Easton—sheds all around a small plot of hard-packed
ground. But the little space was very cleanly swept. Trying to

keep the houses clean is like trying to keep our woodsheds
and barns clean. When a woman is weaving baskets all day
long, how can she keep that room clean in which the straw
and bamboo has to be strewn all over? This woman whom we
saw making the baskets was receiving something like 5 cents
(less than 2 cents our money) per basket, and she could make
7 or 8 a day.

We asked the secretary how much it costs to live a
day. She had no statistics for this locality, but she cited the
findings of some research workers up north. They found that
a family of four could live on 20 cents (about 6 to 7 cents our
money) a day. That compares somewhat with Java where, I
was told, the people were able to live on 10 cents a day, but
the Dutch government was asking them to live on 6 cents and
they were having a hard time of it. I was also told that in Java
the average amount spent for clothes per person in a year was
2.6 cents, which would be less than 2 cents our money. This
was among the natives, of course. It hardly seems possible,
and yet, since many of them go in birthday suits the year
around, it being altogether too warm for much else, and many
others wearing nothing but the one piece of cloth around
the lower part of the body, and probably buying one of those
once in a lifetime, costing possibly 25 or 50 cents, perhaps it's
quite true.

(I always start out writing one thing and end off with
another. I am still in the Chinese village but got down to Java
somehow.)

To go on—one thing that just tickled me all over was the
baby in one of the homes. It sat in a wooden thing that looked
exactly like a very large butter churn. I said "sat;" I mean
"stood!" There was a partition—like a floor, about halfway up,
and on this the child (only some 6 or 8 months old I would
judge) stood, with its head and arms out at the top. It had a

hood on, and a quilt was wrapped around it. But the quilt from the waist down was pulled outside of the churn, and the baby's little behind was absolutely bare—and it was so cold in the house (there are no doors in the doorways—everything wide open) that I was frozen. I said, "Goodness, isn't the baby cold?" They say, "Oh no, we build a fire underneath it." (!) And sure enough, we tilted the churn, and underneath was a little pan in which were some ashes showing that a small charcoal or straw fire had been under it, and they said it was still warm. Where the warmth was I don't know; the ashes looked absolutely white to me. I asked how in the world a child that tiny was expected to <u>stand</u>. The secretary looked at me significantly and said, "They must get used to it." The baby, of course, got frightened with all the people around and began to cry. The sister, who evidently was "minding" the child, just laughed, picked up a single piece of straw that was on the floor and handed it to the child to play with! Imagine an American baby receiving a piece of straw and being content to play with it!

All along here and there we saw lines of "washing," just simply rags—things that we wouldn't even think of putting in a mop because they were both too dirty and too far gone as rags. Cloth shoes that you wondered if they would hold together. I don't know why these people wash their clothing at all; it always seems just as dirty when on the line as when on their bodies. I admire the fact that they do get the things in water, but I'm sure they have no soap, and I doubt if they would have enough hot water. All the wood I saw was simply twigs that had been gathered from a possible tree in the neighborhood, the vines from peas and beans, and straw that couldn't be used for baskets. They use it just to heat the water for tea, and to cook the little rice they use—never for heat.

Gee, when you walk along the streets and see how these poor coolies[7] are dressed (or undressed rather) it makes you wonder how things are ever going to be evened up in the hereafter. We look at the wealthy people at home and wonder why we can't ride around in Packards and wear beautiful gowns, and not have to worry from payday to payday as to rent, taxes, food, etc. When you come out here and visit the back streets or a village, you feel like crawling into your own home barn and calling it a paradise—which it really would be in comparison. Taking into consideration the chopping block, the usual stepladder, and the lawnmower and possibly bench, it certainly would have much more furniture than I saw in any of these houses. And the rake, hoe, spade, shovel, etc. would make our woodsheds look like veritable Curtis & Yale machine shops[8] in comparison. In this particular village, I was told, some of the young girls work in Shanghai factories. They walk to and from work (1½ hours each way), work 12 hours for 6 days and 16 hours on Sundays (because of the change in shift that day), and earn $12 to $15 ($4 to $5 our money) a <u>month</u>. No doubt that has to support the whole family. One girl came up to the secretary and asked about some gloves that she wanted and had asked the secretary to try to get for her. They cost 35 cents, which was more than the girl felt she could afford to pay (about 11 cents our money). Two of us wanted to buy them, but the secretary said it might set a precedent and we had to be very careful. There were other girls in the village that might feel badly. And so it goes.

---

7. Per the *Encyclopedia Britannica*: "(from Hindi *Kuli*, an aboriginal tribal name, or from Tamil *kuli*, "wages'), in usually pejorative European usage, an unskilled laborer or porter usually in or from the Far East hired for low or subsistence wages."

8. Curtis & Yale was a custom manufacturing company in Wausau.

Clara's first months in Shanghai were spent looking for a job and a place to live. By mid-December, she had found both, so she decided to spend her first Christmas away from home with someone she knew from Wausau: Erna Flatter. Erna was a missionary stationed in Yochow,[9] which today is an eleven-hour drive from Shanghai. The first leg of the arduous journey involved Clara's first experience with air travel. Flying in the 1930s was not for the faint of heart. Today's discomforts of air travel pale in comparison to what Clara describes, although the delays and the lack of food are familiar.

Mission Station
Yochow, China
December 17, 1936
My first experience on a plane was anything but heartening. We got to Nanking[10] and waited an hour for better weather. It was pouring; the plane was filled to capacity; no ventilation when the plane stands still; so I got outside and stooped under a wing for an hour or so in a field that was like a swamp. I got my feet soaked to the point where the water bubbled up between my toes when I tried to exercise them; and after I got cold to the point of extinction I went back into the plane and tried to dry my feet by wrapping them up in the steamer rug provided by the steward. I had had breakfast about six that morning and had no more food. The plane was supposed to have arrived at Hankow at 10:55 a.m.; it got there around three that afternoon. We stepped out into an icy blast, rain, and deep mud, and had to walk about half a block to the waiting bus and pack into it two deep. With an empty stomach, and the plane the last lap feeling like a springless

---

9. Yueyang.
10. Nanjing.

oxcart, wallowing from side to side and climbing and falling with sudden jerks, believe you me, I had all I could do to keep from a rendezvous with my breakfast. Anyway, I came into Hankow tired, hungry, somewhat nauseated, awfully wet, terribly cold. Outside of that, I was quite happy.

Erna met Clara in Hankow to accompany her the rest of the way. They spent the night in Hankow[11] and, before daylight the next day, crossed the river in a private launch.

We had to go to the launch down a dark sort of temporary bridge, wait for about a half hour, and then clamber across three "lighters" (sort of flat cargo boats) that were terribly slippery (it having begun to drizzle) and it was pitch dark. Well—skip it. Anyway, we finally got to the other side and it was a pretty long stretch and the launch was loaded down so that I thought the river would pour in over the sides any minute, and the water was rough, and there was no light in the boat, and there were over a dozen of us packed in between dozens and dozens of bags (including a bowl of goldfish!).

The final leg of the journey was an eight-hour train ride, beginning at eight o'clock in the evening. Clara and Erna shared a compartment. Clara seems to have adjusted her expectations regarding cleanliness:

No upholstery; just a long seat running crosswise of the car, and we were given quilts to lay on and fold over ourselves if we wanted to sleep—and the looks of the quilts! Well, since I've been on this trek, I have learned to shut off my imagination, or I wouldn't eat or drink, or sleep or breathe.

---

11. Hangzou.

Yochow greeted Clara with the coldest weather of the year. Once settled in her room, she said the icy wind blew right in because the windows "fit like a saddle on a cow!" Clara was sanguine about most discomforts, but she frequently complained about the cold, as mentioned throughout her description of activities surrounding this visit. One of the first activities she described is an authentic Chinese dinner. She stated that she wanted to record her "thoughts and reactions (to say nothing of my actions!) in detail." The dinner was held at the home of a friend of Erna's, James Tang, who, just to emphasize how much networking occurred between missionaries and the YWCA, had been a guest at Alexander Lodge, a YWCA gathering spot on the river outside of Wausau, for what Clara described as an "eventful night when we had two or three gentlemen as guests." The following is an excerpt of a letter addressed to the Blue Triangle Club:

Mission Station
Yochow, China
December 1936
There was no snow on the ground, but it was very cold.
(If this were a letter to one of my pals, it would have been
"darned" cold; if to a lumberjack, it would have been even
colder than that! But this is a formal letter, so just dress
up the "very" a little bit.) We ran across the compound all
huddled and hunched up, clear to the very wall on the far
side. It was so dark I thought we actually were knocking on
an outside wall door or gateway, but a door opened and we
stepped into a tiny cement-floored room. It was such a small
room, but even so, it contained a rather large desk, several
square severe chairs, a teensy-weensy stove with a firepot
about the size of a basketball, and in one corner a Christmas
tree, put up just that afternoon for our benefit. It was a small

shrub-like pine with rather long needles, trimmed with what we used to make in kindergarten back in the 90's, gold paper stars, and kumquats hung on by store string. That's all the trimmings. Around the base of the tree were three or four pots of geraniums, with newspaper tied around each pot.

On arrival we were each handed a small bowl of tea. I say "bowl" which means really a handle-less cup, but not quite as large in diameter as our cups. As far as I have observed, these preliminary hand outs are used by the guests to warm their hands. I have seldom seen guests drinking it. If after a time the guests are not yet all assembled, the hostess will come around and take your bowl, empty the cooled tea, and fill it with hot again.

Finally the last stragglers came in, got their hands warmed on their bowls of tea, and we were ushered into the next very small room that boasted only a round dining room table and a crude buffet. Narrow benches served as chairs; the room would not have been large enough had we had regular chairs. The only fire was a pan of charcoal placed under the table. They are really low four-legged tables—possibly 8" high with a top some 18" square into which a hole is cut in the middle. The pan of glowing charcoal is set into the hole. . . .

At each place was a deep saucer, a porcelain spoon, a pair of pewter chopsticks, and a small bowl of tea. The center of the table held but one dish, filled with dried watermelon seeds. There's a trick in trying to crack these seeds open with the teeth, seeds I wasted before I got into the swing of it. I think these seeds are served invariably at every feast. You nibble them before the first dish or "course" is brought in; you nibble them between each course; you nibble while waiting for the others to finish; in fact you nibble all the time, and you could go on nibbling the rest of the night and never know you had eaten anything. In public restaurants you throw the seed shells over your shoulder onto the floor; after a feast the table looks bad, but the floor looks worse.

After grace was said the food began appearing on the table. First came a dish containing meatballs of some sort, beche de mer, sliced bamboo, and kidney. Each guest helped himself, reaching to the middle of the table with chopsticks. We kept our coats on. Reaching to the middle of the table, across a half dozen greasy dishes with wide fur coat sleeves is a lesson in dexterity. Next came a dish of shredded bamboo; then a whole chicken, which was expertly carved with chopsticks by a Chinese girl, superintendent of the school. After the chicken there was another meat dish—licorice flavored beef. This was followed, to my surprise, by two bowls of hot water, in which I was instructed to wash my porcelain spoon. That seemed to signify that we would start all over again because along came a sweet dish—lotus seeds; and another meat dish—pork balls with Chinese cabbage; then another dish of Chinese cabbage with dried shrimps. Just before the last came in, a large charcoal cooker was set amongst all these other dishes—a sort of chafing dish—containing boiling soup with noodles, Chinese cabbage, and small "silver fish." These tiny fish were clear white, and you could hardly distinguish them from the noodles except that they were only some 2" to 3" long and their tiny black beady eyes stuck out and gave you an accusing look just as you opened your mouth. I shut my eyes and they shook down on the ensuing shudder. They didn't taste so hot either. This country dotes on dried fish of all sorts, and the odor is terrible, and the taste, as far as I've experienced, isn't much better.

At about this time we were given a bowl of rice, too, and two small dishes of pickled turnips and peppers (very hot) were brought in. I've tasted some of the pickled things here and some of them will take the skin right off your teeth. These people can eat hotter things than I've ever seen done anywhere. And last, but not least, on came one of my by-now favorite Chinese dishes—a whole Mandarin fish in ginger sauce. When the fish is served whole, everybody jabs into it with chopsticks and in no time there's merely the skeleton left. To me this always seems so brutal, but I'll get used to it in time.

I understand the Chinese idea is to serve enough dishes so that every guest will find at least a few to his liking. And no one is expected to eat much of each dish, altho they will press you and almost force you to second and third helpings; your only recourse being to let the food remain untouched on your dish, which is perfectly all right.

As the dishes are placed on the table the previous one was pushed aside and the last placed into the middle. The table began to get awfully crowded, and the congealed greasiness of the first plates didn't add to the general aspect of the table. At long last we arose; were given steaming hot towels to wipe our hands and lips; and then ushered back to the living room—handed the inevitable bowl of tea—and polite conversation ensued, all in Chinese, with translations being slopped to me on the side.

I didn't envy the girls in the kitchen (I believe daughters) who had to clean up the table. With the soups, gravy and sauces dripped all over the cloth; the watermelon seeds strewn every which way; the cooling dishes a mass of mess—I was glad to depart from the scene.

Finally we bade our host and hostess goodnight and left.

The highlight of this visit for Clara was attending a Chinese wedding, which was held in a small village seven miles from Yo-chow. Getting there was another transportation adventure.

December 1936

A morning or two after arriving here, I found among the
mail on a table a wedding invitation, printed with bright red
Chinese characters on a large pink card. It being very near
Christmas with much to do at the school, Ernie felt she could
not attend and suggested I go in her stead. Our Chinese
pastor was to officiate and Miss Hoy was to be the organist,
so Mrs. Whitener, the wife of the superintendent of our
compound, decided that she would also go, taking her two
young boys with her. She, her older son, and one of the men
of the compound started out on bicycles. The Chinese pastor,
a guest of his (a Chinese man high in military circles of that
district), Miss Hoy, the younger boy, and I went in rickshas.
We made quite a grand parade.

There was no snow on the ground, but the weather
was pretty cold. As far as protection from the weather is
concerned, a ricksha is as effective as a highchair on the High
Bridge[12] in mid-winter. Fortunately, just before we started,
the American hospital nurse sent a servant over to our house
with her fur-lined Chinese garment—floor length, high
collar, and long sleeves. I had all the clothes I could possibly
put on—heavy undies, wool sox over silk, heavy woolen
dress, sweater, this fur-lined garment, and my fur coat. Ernie
had a brass hot-water bottle filled with boiling water for my
hands and feet.

The 7-mile ride was an exciting thrill for me. Miss Hoy
kept calling back to me, trying to give me an idea of things
we were passing. At one place was a high narrow tower, built
on the order of a pagoda. It was solid masonry from bottom
to top with the exception of a rather small hole about 7 or 8

---

12. The High Bridge spanned the Wisconsin River, upriver from the railroad
depot in Wausau.

feet above the ground. That is known as the "baby tower." It was the place where the Chinese of that locality used to throw their unwanted girl babies![13] As we passed small groups of houses, we could catch glimpses of life within. Most of these houses were of mud and straw—no doors, even though it was freezing cold, and no fires either. Often we would see a small blaze of charcoal in a shallow brass or iron container, with all the family huddling over it trying to warm their hands. In one hut I saw the family sitting around a terribly crude table, and a large cat was perched on one edge, evidently perfectly at home and not being molested one bit. In another home I saw some pigs in one corner; and the man of the household was sitting working at something near the door.

We passed a shipyard that made me gasp with admiration. Only junks and large row-boats were made there (nothing like the *Queen Mary* or *Normandie*), but the beautiful large timbers in the process of being shaped and assembled would make any retail yard man at home green with envy. I don't know a great deal about lumber, but enough so that I fairly thrilled to see those huge timbers. And the men about that yard weren't lagging either; it was the most serious and most decided looking group of workmen I've seen yet this side of Suez. I didn't see a one of them stopping to stare at our queer looking parade, and we got plenty of stares all along the way.

The going was quite rough in spots and twice I held my breath when we crossed large flat stones laid across streams and the rickshas swayed like some of the ships I've been on. But we landed safely, going down the narrowest, dirtiest, smelliest streets imaginable the last stretch.

---

13. "The killing of female babies was a widespread practice in China going back centuries, though it was outlawed in 1935, just before Clara arrived in Shanghai." See Bernice J. Lee, "Female Infanticide in China," *Historical Reflections* 8.3 (1981).

Clara's reference to the *Queen Mary* and *Normandie* is evidence of her awareness of contemporary world events. The *Queen Mary* was a British ocean liner that set sail in 1936; the *Normandie* was a French ocean liner, known for its lavish appointments, that took her maiden voyage in 1935. During World War II, the *Queen Mary* was converted into a troopship, and the *Normandie* was seized by the United States in New York and caught fire while being converted into a troopship.

In Clara's detailed account of the wedding, she is both a spectator, making wry observations, and an appreciative participant. Her sarcastic brand of humor and powers of description are fully on display for the entertainment of her readers. But underlying her arch commentary, I detect her delight in being part of an authentic cultural experience.

When we neared the church in which the wedding was to take place, yards of firecrackers were set off. They were accompanied by cymbals that made a deafening noise when pounded with more vim and vigor than a Yale-Harvard football match, a drum, and a few horns which set up a howl like I've never heard anywhere. I don't know where they got those brass horns nor whether they were trying to get any tune out of them—I thought perhaps all of them were um-pahs gone double-flat. I don't know what "hell let loose" sounds like, but if "March of Time"[14] ever wants to dramatize it, I strongly urge them to hire this wedding band, the cymbal ensemble, and the firecrackers! Just as Miss Hoy began playing the Lohengrin wedding march on the wheeziest organ

---

14. *The March of Time* was a short newsreel series shown in American movie theaters between 1935 and 1951, produced by Roy E. Larsen, Louis de Rochemont, and Richard de Rochemont (New York: Time, Inc.).

on this green earth, lo and behold, those ungodly instruments blared forth in all their glory! I was almost convulsed.

But to go back a ways, we arrived. I was so cold that I could barely stumble through the small church, and into the rooms built at the back of it where the pastor and his family live. It was their eldest son who was being married. Being a Christian, he wanted the wedding to be carried out in the true Christian style. However, the bride's parents, not being Christian and being more or less well-to-do, insisted on a number of Chinese customs. Result: One final conglomeration that would make our movie comedies look like funerals.

As I said before, and before that, I was desperately cold. So I was hustled into the—well, dining room, I suppose—a very tiny rock-floored room where a low table stood under which was a shallow pan of glowing charcoal. I held my hands and feet over that pan until the ceremony began.

While we had been riding in rickshas, the bride had been coming the same way in her wedding chair, sealed in tight, carried on the shoulders of a number of coolies. There was a band (if you wish to call it that) and a number of people in the "parade" with her, carrying a number of symbolic things. One was a goose, symbol of fidelity. These people were all dressed for their parts, too, a regular circus parade. The chair was bright red, and when it was first sighted while still some distance away, everybody got excited and all was chaos for a while.

The chair was brought right up through the front hallway of the church, while the blare of the musical (!) instruments and the crashing of the cymbals deafened everybody. And to top it all off, a barrage of large firecrackers was set off right in the hallway!

Then the bridegroom unsealed the front door of the chair and helped his bride out—a tiny person in a pink gown and veil, pink stockings, pink slippers, gaudy headdress, much-crushed artificial spray of flowers. She staggered and had to be fairly held up as she slowly walked down the aisle, while two little flower girls in pink walked ahead and sprinkled flowers along the way. (Later the bride said she was very dizzy from that 7-mile trek in an air-less chair.) During the processional, the band tried to put the half Nelson on the organ. But the ushers finally hushed them up.

Everybody crowded into the church after the bride, standing on the benches, stretching forward—oh, it was just too funny for words. Even a large tan hound kept pacing in and around the benches all during the performance. But finally the couple got to the platform, and the two pastors were there, one middleman (in this case a woman)[15] was seated in her specified place (the other middleman could not attend for some reason or other), and a hymn was announced and sung. On the left wall toward the front was a large piece of red paper on which was written the plan for the ceremony. And for each and every act, a young man, who was evidently master of ceremonies, would call off or announce what was on that program. Everything was in Chinese of course (I was the only person in the village that day I guess who couldn't speak or understand it), so I no doubt missed a lot of interesting things.

The wedding rings were signets, and the bride and groom each received a wedding certificate, sealed with each other's signet, sealed by the middleman, sealed by the pastor, sealed by the bride's family and sealed by the groom's family. (The bride's parents did not attend the wedding; that is not done in China. But her sister was one of the bridesmaids, which

---

15. Families hired middlemen to negotiate the size of the dowry and wedding details.

was a distinctly modern touch.) The couple had to bow to the bridegroom's father, the middleman, the congregation, and to each other—each time the act being announced by the master of ceremonies much as a square-dance announcer does.

Well, the wedding came to an end, stopping as abruptly as a game of "Run Sheep Run" when the curfew rings at home, and everybody exited to the living rooms, the bride going directly to her small room upstairs where she modestly stayed until she could revive a little. Later the husband went up and then both came down to thank us for coming. Later, we all went outside and the wedding pictures were taken by the city photographer from Yochow. And the whole crowd was included in the wedding picture!

We went up to see the bride's room before she came. The "double happiness" character was cut out of red paper and placed everywhere. All her gifts of furniture, etc., were placed in their proper places. On the bed were sprigs of cedar and dates—both to bring many sons. They asked Mrs. Whitener to sit on the bed for luck, since she has 3 sons. I want to add parenthetically that among the guests was one woman, 36 years old, who was the mother of <u>eleven</u> children; 6 sons and 2 daughters living. She had her first child when 18 years old. (All right, Clara, say it!)

Then the feast! I think there were 17 or 20 dishes. Since I was a sort of special guest, as a world tourist and Ernie's guest and proxy, everybody waited for me to dip my chopsticks into whatever dish was placed on the table. They commented on my dexterity with the chopsticks, and no sooner had they said something than a large piece of flabby, greasy, fish-stomach plopped right into the V of my fur collar. (Oh, yes, we all kept our coats and hats on; the doors were wide open, and the thermometer on the wall registered 40 degrees.)

The people were all perfectly lovely to me. I felt perfectly

at home; they were as cordial as could be. When we left, the
mother of the household saw to it that our hot-water bottles
were filled; the father saw to it that our rickshas were ready
and our coolies paid; the groom saw to it that we were all
well tucked in with robes. The entire day was a lovely one,
and despite the physical discomforts, it was one of the most
interesting days I've had on the trip—and I've had some
mighty thrilling ones.

As Clara's visit drew to a close, she wrote about the logistical
challenge of returning to Shanghai and struck a few other familiar
themes.

Mission Station
Yochow
Christmas Eve
December 24, 1936
I landed a job in Shanghai and have to report for work on
the 28th, so in order to get back on time, I have to leave here
at 11 p.m. on Christmas night. I don't relish the trip one little
bit. I am at last evidently and definitely in China. . . . When
I got to Hong Kong, I was told that it wasn't China; same
with Kowloon—across the bay. The one part of Canton also
wasn't China, and Shanghai, I was told, wasn't China; AND
when I got to Hankow, I was told the same thing. I finally
despaired of ever being in China. But at Yochow I've met it
with a vengeance. . . . I am a little apprehensive about that
trip on the night train alone to Hankow, and I won't arrive
until 7 or 8 in the morning, where I expect a man from the
Lutheran Mission Home to meet me at the station. The
interior of China is one place where you don't meet the
English language in stations, post offices, etc. I am hoping
to catch the Saturday afternoon plane which will land me

in Shanghai about 5 o'clock (4 hours later). That will give me Sunday to rest. The Sunday plane leaves before the morning pulls in or I could spend another day here.

I attended the Christmas Eve services in the church here in the compound this evening. The Christmas tree is a squatty, bushlike pine tree, trimmed with Easter lilies (!), gold paper stars and chains, and red and green paper chains. It really looked quite nice. Then chains and paper bells were festooned from the ceiling and some very lovely white stars were placed at strategic points here and there.

The band from the local orphanage (a county institution) played a few selections—and did they play! There were about 3 pieces—mostly alto horns; something that looked like a cornet and one that looked like a clarinet but sounded more like a bagpipe, and then a bass and a snare drum. They didn't play the white, black, or cracks—they played all around the piano. Double flats and sharps had no terrors for them. But the little snare drummer was superb. He is a marvel.

And now I shall have to hop because my feet are getting cold and I want to go warm them. Anyway, the piano bench is filled with gifts (all the local people remembered me along with Miss Traub and Ernie, of course), and I want to open them. We have a grand garland of holly which the "boy" gathered the other day, and our tree is a cedar about 7 feet tall, but no trimmings as Miss Traub forgot where she put them last year and hasn't been able to locate them. What a Christmas! But I'm happy and having a deeply interesting time.

3

Shanghai

Clara's job at the American Consulate in the very international city of Shanghai was an ideal learning opportunity. She kept up a brisk correspondence, giving us insight into her insatiable curiosity about the world and its inhabitants.

Shanghai, China
January 6, 1937
Dearest Irma:
To give you the atmosphere of this letter first of all: I am sitting at the typewriter of the Assistant Commercial Attache—a Remington noiseless, which is honest-to-goodness as nearly noiseless as anything I've ever run across. It is shortly after one o'clock and I have a full ¾ of an hour before anybody will return. I brought my lunch today instead of going out after it, as I've done heretofore. One other girl does the same thing. A very young girl who several years ago decided she wanted to go places and struck out for Shanghai, got herself a job, of which I gather she has had plenty of various denominations since, and is still here, after four years more or less. She says she may go back home next year or so. How she manages to exist is more than I can see, on her income. But she's one of these happy-go-lucky sorts

and I think is getting enjoyment out of it in her own way—
boyfriend and all things included.

There are so many interesting stories connected with
almost everyone you run into out here, i.e. those from other
countries. There are two other girls here whose personal
stories I haven't found out yet; that'll come later. The girl
whom I replaced had the most unusual background. She calls
herself an American although she was born in Russia (if I
remember correctly), raised in Shanghai, with a year or more
of Japan thrown in, higher education in Paris (claims she's a
graduate of the Sorbonne), and has since lived here. Her only
claim to American citizenship is that her father, she says, was
an American. (Now in that case just what nationality would
you call her? She has never set foot in the USA. I'm sorry I
didn't ask her from whom she obtained her passport to go to
Paris.)

Oh, before I forget, these offices—main and six private,
all of nice dimensions—are to me very grand. In four of
them, including the one I'm in, there are large, very heavy
Peiping[1] rugs—dull rose color on a sort of mellow grey (no
doubt the sun has put the "dull" and "mellow" in it). The
walls are done in cream color, and the woodwork, desks,
files, furniture are all dark brown. In this office there is
also a leather-upholstered settee, full length, on which the
above mentioned little girl (she is tiny) sleeps every noon (a
positive necessity, I gather, due to late nights).

I'd like to tell Guy Gooding[2] about the rugs. I always
wanted one for my office and he would just grin every time
I'd ask him and say, "Yea, wouldn't a nice Oriental rug look
lovely after a couple men from the shop stalked through the

---

1. Sometimes spelled Peking, now known as Beijing.
2. Guy Gooding, president of Wisconsin Box, was Clara's former boss.

yard and came in and wiped their feet off on it, with all the
mud and snow, etc., not counting the nails in their shoes,
s'more, s'more, etc., etc."

I might add that in the office in which I am at present
located there are three of us: the assistant commercial attache
(a peach—fat, well along in years; I deeply admire his power
of concentration and am secretly studying it), a Chinese boy
(graduate of a highly rated local university), and yours truly.
From this Chinese (I shouldn't say "boy;" he's married; but
most Chinese are so small-statured that I think of them as
boys until I learn they have about six or twelve children)
fellow I expect to learn a lot and derive no little amount of
information, interest and amusement. And I know he's getting
the same from me. He's awfully nice and about breaks his
neck to do little things for me, and when I ask him questions
about China, he goes on and on.

The arrival of the Chinese New Year was a rich opportunity
for Clara to delve into cultural beliefs and customs.

Shanghai, China
Feb. 4, 1937
Dearest Irma:
Gee, Kiddo, I wish you were here with me! There are so many
things to do and so many interesting things to learn about
China, and it would be such fun doing them together! Just
now the Chinese New Year is in the offing—Feb. 11, 12, and
13; we have those days off and Miss Hinkley and I are going to
Hangchow,[3] a little southwest of Shanghai. Already the place
here is taking on a festive air; day after day one sees Chinese
riding along in rickshas holding huge bunches of Chinese

---

3. Hangzhou.

"heavenly bamboo"—a sort of tall bushy plant that gets huge clusters of bright red berries—somewhat on the order of our elderberries; looks a little like them when their berries are in the red state. But the leaves are longer, thinner, and more feathery looking, consequently. Another flower used a great deal is the national flower, the mai wha (may wha). It blossoms before the leaves come out—some are pink like our apple blossoms and some are yellow. I would compare them with our apple blossoms, which also come out before the leaves do, but these flowers are only ⅓ to ½ as large and they hug the stem very tightly. It's the prettiest thing when just two or three sprigs are in a vase. The pink ones they sell as small trees, twisting them into zig-zags.[4]

And there's a lot of firecracker shooting every night, big ones and little ones. It seems that 10 days or 2 weeks before the festivities begin, the Chinese send up the Kitchen God to the spirit world to report on all the household activities of the past year. In order that he may say sweet things, they put sorghum on his lips. (I'm gradually trying to learn a little about their gods, but it's difficult because everybody seems to have a little different story to tell. I suppose it could be compared with our own different interpretations of our Bible stories. But I'll get there, I'm sure, if I keep on asking enough people.)

February 5, 1937
I learned a little more about this Kitchen God last night, so here goes. He is one of the 5 gods worshipped in the family shrines. (The other 4 are the Door God, the Gate God, the Well God, and the Chamber God.) The Kitchen God (a

---

4. The flowers on Clara's stationery (see photograph on page 90) are likely mai wha.

picture, of course) hangs in the home all year around. Last
night was the night that he was "escorted" from the shrine
in the sedan-chair (also of paper), and then thrown into
a bonfire with a large quantity of "spirit money," thereby
transferring him from this world to the next. To show you
how modernity has crept in, the Chinese now not only send
the god in a sedan-chair or wheelbarrow, but they also use
paper airplanes, cars, and boats. A short account in a paper
last evening says the stores were experiencing heavy sales
yesterday. . . .

The Kitchen God returns the morning of New Year's Day
after reporting to the "Heavenly Emperor" on the merits
and demerits of his particular household. In some cases
special sacrifices are offered before he leaves the earth, and
they flatter him with sticky sweets, fruits, etc. (I understand
the "sticky" is chosen so that his lips will be slightly stuck,
preventing him from speaking too much in paradise.)

I wish I could have seen some of the ceremonies, but near
us the Chinese are too modern, or perhaps Christianized,
or they go to the homes of their parents for the rites. I saw
some paper creations in a store yesterday that for color
would knock your eyes out—Chinese red and cerise pink
generously thrown together—but for workmanship they'd
arouse the imagination of anybody, especially anybody as
interested in that sort of thing as you and I are.

Clara had heard Hangzhou described as "heaven on earth," so
she was eager to visit and report back on it. But the plight of those
whose lives are far from "heavenly" was never far from her mind.

129/32 Avenue Haig
Shanghai, China
February 18, 1937

Dearest Lyd:

My trip to Hangchow (about 4 hours ride south of Shanghai) was as delightful as it could be. The first two days we had rain, and just a dusting of snow, so we couldn't do much in the way of walking around. But Saturday morning we started out for one of the hills and didn't return until late in the afternoon. I'll never forget that day. It was my first trip to a monastery—the Ling Yin, which is sprawled all over a hill. One part of the hill is just covered with a heavy growth of tall bamboo, and the trunks were such a heavenly green that I just couldn't believe I was looking at something outside a painting. (I found that human nature again proved alike all over the world; on many trees were cut the names, or something of visitors—Chinese characters all over. "Fools' names, like fools' faces, etc.") The hill is a very high one, I think higher than Rib Hill, and very steep. The monks have done a splendid job of stone-stepping in the pathways. Near the bottom is a series of temples and living quarters (for the monks), and then going up a series of steps to the left is a temple to the God of Wealth; while a series of steps to the right leads to the very top and there is a temple of, goodness, I don't know whom. I don't think I'll even try to get all these gods straightened out. I no sooner think I have the Buddhist ones somewhat in line, then comes another string of Taoist ones, and then there seems to be another group, like the Kitchen God, the Door God, etc. that are just gods—whether Buddhist, Taoist, blank-ist, or what, I don't know.

The temples look like huge barns, but of course with beautifully carved things outside, and lovely roofs. There are usually large openings in the front and back walls, and perhaps one or two regular sized doors at the sides. In the center is usually a most elaborate altar-like affair with the most exquisite carvings of the most grotesque gods you

ever saw. In one of those temples at the foot of the hill were
four large gods, about as high as a telephone post, and
proportionately, as big all around. We took many pictures and
I'll be sending some home to Irma; they will give you a better
idea than my vague descriptions.

One large temple in the city has a series of large carvings
and "scenes" along both sides showing the punishments of
hell. To us they were extremely amusing. One shows a man
being sawed in two; he is standing on his head, and the man
with the saw has commenced between his legs, sawing him
down the middle! Another shows the branch of a tree on
which a huge snake is coiled waiting for the sinners that are
forced to climb a ladder up to the limb! These scenes are
all done with small statues, and some have become rather
broken and blurred with age, but there still remains enough
to get the general idea from scene to scene. Imagine going to
church every Sunday and passing the vivid portrayals of hell.
I think I'd stay away from church.

I think I saw another hell over in Bangkok in one of the
very beautiful temples; but it was beautifully done. Well,
anyway, I'm getting some good ideas. I don't know why these
people seem to be so anxious to portray hell all the time and
not heaven, and their gods are such awful-looking affairs
that I wonder what the poor sinners are thinking about.
Goodness, their everyday life out here is hell enough (that
is, the poor class) that the temples ought to give them the
brightest views of a possible heaven!

Clara's social consciousness was frequently awakened at the
same time that she became increasingly attuned to how perspective colors one's view of events. She followed current events in
China as well as in the United States. In the February 4 letter
to Irma, she contrasted how Lelia, who is "very much in love

with China and is keenly anxious that everybody coming into the country receive the best impressions," downplayed street executions there with how other acquaintances sensationalized street violence in the United States that was related to the seamen's strike. Clara concluded the letter with this statement about nationalism: "I guess when it comes to brass tacks, it's a case of keeping one's own national skeleton tightly sealed in a closet and listening for the rattle through the other fellow's closet door." Her letters provide a unique window on the world at this period of history, making clear that one's interpretation of events is affected by one's perch. She strived to be candid and forthright, which is, in part, what makes her letters so valuable.

Shanghai, China
February 23, 1937
Yes, it's true about China inflicting capital punishment on
drug addicts. As I understand it, they are given two trials;
on the third offense out they go. I wish they would do the
same with some of the poor, diseased, crippled, desperately
miserable beggars that one sees on the street day after
day—and the <u>men</u> who are responsible for putting into the
world a dozen or more children with not a copper to support
them; in fact, putting their children out to beg for their own
support as well as for the parents. Would you believe it true
that parents would put a baby in a large earthenware jar and
keep it there until fully grown so that it would be a hopeless
mis-shapen creature, just in order that it would draw the
pity of passers-by and support the parents by begging?[5] And
when an organization found a poor wretch with cataracts

---

5. Though Clara is relating hearsay in this letter, intentional disfigurement
   of children by exploiters for purposes of sending them out to beg occurs
   around the world even today.

on his eyes, destitute, begging, and took him to a surgeon,
operated, restored sight, health, life; that the relatives would
turn around and sue that organization for support because
it took their only means of support away from them in the
shape of a woe-begone human wretch who at least could beg
and turn the money over to them? Well, those are true tales.
I saw a horrible sight in the Chinese City yesterday—two
children, mere infants, squatted down in the middle of the
narrow, muddy, cold, jagged pavement, and in front of them
a tiny baby flat on its back on a dirty straw mat; all of them
filthy, diseased, ragged! You know I just felt I couldn't do any
praying last night; I could see those three babies in front of
me, and I just didn't have the nerve to ask for "daily bread"
when I'm always more or less overfed and there's always
food to spare in the house. How could I say "Thy will be
done" when surely His will is that those youngsters should
somehow be taken care of and I was doing nothing about it.
What business had I asking to be "delivered from evil"—I,
who up to now, have always led a sheltered life—when these
poor youngsters are helpless right in the midst of the most
evil things in the world.

I don't know, maybe I'm cockeyed, but I didn't see
anything in India like that. Anyhow, it's warm over there,
and the youngsters don't have to shiver on cold pavement;
they do get sunshine. I get so exasperated with China; the
government to me seems so desperately passive. Here's
Chang Hsueh Liang who kidnapped Chiang Kai Shek, the
most important man in China at the time, and he has not
only been set absolutely free, but, I believe, the newspaper
yesterday or today states he is slated for an important
post. (The Legislature is meeting at Nanking right now—
somewhat on the order of our session of Congress.)

I simply don't get it at all. And when I say so to the

Chinese in this office, he invariably answers that it's no use for the Western or American mind to try to understand the Chinese mind. In other words, the thing itself is not queer; it's just because we don't understand the workings of the Chinese mind; the working is perfectly all right and we would see it in that light if we could <u>understand</u> it. In other words, when a man kills another man, he isn't a murderer and he did nothing wrong—if we understand his mind, reason, logic, and motive!

∼

Given the enrichment Clara found in the Wausau YWCA's Blue Triangle Club, it's not surprising that she sought to create a similar club within the Shanghai YWCA. She saw an opportunity to enliven an existing club and, with a missionary zeal, soon made an impact.

Shanghai, China
February 23, 1937
I attended a meeting of girl's council at the International YWCA building last evening. It seems that the international department of the Y here has but one club of business girls. It's about as active as an extinct volcano; I'm trying to cause an eruption. I was <u>so</u> amused when I walked in. They were planning a dinner. There were 2 Chinese girls, one Korean, one Belgian, one English, one Polish, one American, one Japanese, and, I believe, one Russian. Just as I came in, I heard them suggesting names of what I took to be vaudeville performers. They wanted something snappy and funny; something that would be a "drawing card—or else nobody will come." A short style show was discussed at length. Between cigarette smoke and vaudeville performers, any idea I had about doing something in the way of organizing

a Shanghai Blue Triangle Club became almost extinct. They
have absolutely no idea of the YWCA. A Chinese dance was
suggested, the "scarf dance" which is oh so lovely, and the
Polish girl (a real live wire) said it would be all right, but she
insisted that it be cut down to not a second more than 10
minutes! And they didn't want too much of the "intellectual"
at the supper—something funny rather. And they insisted
on having a speaker that everybody knew so that she would
"draw."

I do want to do something for the girls who are wandering
around in this big city with no place to go evenings, no
place to get acquainted with anybody—the church Sunday
mornings seems to me to be sadly lacking in the girls of my
age—or I would say from 20 to 30. (I always forget that 40 is
supposed to be "middle age.") There are no clubs at the Y as
we have them.

As I say, I want to do something, but it really takes full
time to get something into the swing, and with foreign
secretaries out here who say flatly, "Oh, we've tried that; it
can't be done in Shanghai." Well, it is discouraging to say the
least. I know Miss Hinkley could have swung it, and we had
made plans, but now with her up in Peiping, it is no go, and
the New Zealand girl who is going to take her place seems
to have about as much enthusiasm as the average British
female. I may be mistaken but the outlook isn't very bright.
Anyway, I butted into this council meeting and they took
me in quite graciously and said they would be awfully glad
to have me stick with them. Most of the girls are more or
less sophisticated, the type that would simply freeze out any
timid girl; all of them seemed to know Shanghai very well,
so I gathered they had been here for some time. At least I felt
pretty much the small town, unsophisticated lady. But I'm so
anxious to get going that I talked loudly in order to drown

the quake in my voice. (You know how terribly bashful and
reticent I am!)

Clara's thoughts were never far from the Wausau YWCA and
its Blue Triangle Club. The tone of this letter, addressed directly
to the club, seems less spontaneous than those addressed to its
individual members. She sounds intolerant and seems to work
too hard to be clever. She also rebukes herself in the letter, so
perhaps the early part of it hints at what the members might find
entertaining.

Shanghai, China
March 15, 1937
Now, how shall I address you? "Dear Blue Trianglers"
won't do; it sounds too Ike Waltonian.[6] That wouldn't be
original anyhow. I'm getting some perfectly super-intelligent
suggestions on the sidelines by this friend of Miss Blandin's
with whom I'm living. "Dear Pals of the Blue Triangle" and
"Dear Kids," a fair example of what happens to a secretarial
mind away off here where the men make a mad dash for the
bus door, grab all the available seats and stare with marvelous
indifference at the women dangling from the straps (and the
way these buses are driven, you do just that—dangle; the
Man on the Flying Trapeze would get seasick hanging from
one of those straps).

Well, it seems that I've gotten this letter started without
a salutation—and I'll let it go at that. Oriental indifference, I
fear, is beginning to descend upon my super-critical nature.
Coping with floods[7] isn't nearly as hopeless as trying to

---

6. Izaak Walton was a well-known outdoorsman who wrote *The Compleat
   Angler* (London: Richard Marriot, 1653).
7. A reference to the floods of the Ohio and Mississippi Rivers in January
   and February of 1937.

cope with the Oriental in trying to induce discipline, speed (groans!), routine, etc. You can eventually dam a flood, but all the damning in the world won't help you with a coolie.

(That's not quite fair. I've gotten some very good service from coolies, and if I were they I think I'd simply lay me down and die. I simply cannot reconcile myself to the way coolies are treated here in China, not by foreigners, but by their own countrymen. They work so hard, and get so little. My general idea of China is that it is "hard." But I haven't been to Peiping yet, and from all reports, I have come to the conclusion that Peiping is just a few steps this side of heaven. I am looking forward with great anticipation to a visit or stay there.)

Really, now, it's time I got down to brass tacks. Going around in a circle is my favorite hobby these days. Yes, I know I'm liable to get dizzy, but as long as I can still read a map I'll feel safe to go along.

The brass tacks: Thank you, individually and collectively, for the money order! I should have written a letter of thanks months ago, and I don't understand what happened to my sense of responsibility. Not until I received a letter from Irma the other day did it dawn on me that one usually thanks people from whom one receives gifts! What I am going to buy I don't know. The lingerie here in Shanghai about melts my heart; I've sent several things home which perhaps Irma can bring to one of the meetings to show you. I think that's what I will apply the $7 on. Oh, dear, there are so many extremely lovely things to buy!

This rambling will get me nowhere. So I'm holding out my hand showing that my mind's turning a corner. Now, then!

Such frivolity does not appear in upcoming letters, as the looming war arrives on her doorstep.

4

The French Concession

In the spring of 1937, Clara moved to the French Concession, one of two foreign settlements in Shanghai. The International Settlement and the French Concession had been populated for a century by refugees from natural disasters and human conflicts. Encompassing six square miles with a population of two million in 1937, these two settlements were protected from invasion because of their "extraterritorial" status.[1]

5 Avenue Petain
Shanghai, China
April 9, 1937
Dearest Lyd:
The other morning I went over to the neighbor's house to wait for him (I ride to work with him every morning), and as I sat on the steps I felt something brushing against me. I turned to find a large black and white cat, which I proceeded to fondle and pet for all I was worth. . . . When the neighbor came out, I asked if it was his cat; he said it belonged to

---

1. See Christian Henriot, "August 1937: War and Death En Masse of Civilians," July 2015, Virtual Shanghai Project, Lyon Institute of East Asian Studies: www.virtualshanghai.net/Texts/Articles?ID=130.

General Chiang Kai Chek who lives next door! I didn't know
I was petting the cat of probably the greatest man in China
today! (Gettin' up in the world!)

Clara was right to think of her neighbor as the greatest man
in China. *Time* magazine named General Chiang Kai-shek and
Madame Chiang Kai-shek Man and Wife of the Year in 1937 for
unifying China and giving it a national consciousness. The magazine went on to say, "No woman in the West holds so great a
position as Mme Chiang Kai-shek holds in China."[2] Yet *Time*
referred to her as a wife rather than the political partner she was.
It is worth noting that Madame Chiang, also known as Soong
Mei-Ling, was a supporter of the Shanghai YWCA, often engaged
in fundraising on its behalf.

Clara was enjoying a peaceful existence, living in a safe area,
working at the American Consulate, and making her mark on
the YWCA. By May 1937, Clara had accomplished her intent of
creating a Blue Triangle–type club at the YWCA in Shanghai. A
clipping from a Shanghai newspaper with the headline "Business
Girl's Club Organized" indicates that "more than 20 girls met for
the second time at the YWCA, 999 Bubbling Well Road, to hear a
talk given by Miss Clara H. Pagel on English history. A general discussion followed on current historical happenings, including the
Coronation and the various ceremonial significances attached."[3]
An election took place, and Clara was made president. According
to the article, the club "has come into existence as a result of Miss
Pagel's suggesting at the recent Business Girl's Banquet that there
be organized a club, open to all and every Shanghai business girl,
for the promotion of general fellowship." The bimonthly meetings
included debates, lectures, excursions, and discussions of current

2. "International: Man & Wife of the Year," *Time*, January 3, 1938.
3. Clipped from a Tuesday, May 18, 1937, Shanghai newspaper (name not
   identified) by Clara and enclosed in one of her letters.

topics. The club was named The Keys because nearly all the members were "stenographers or at least typists of varying rank; it also conveys the idea of the organization being a 'key' to greater opportunities and new friendships." I'm sure Alma Blandin was very proud of Clara.

Even as tensions between China and Japan were heating up, Clara assumed that, if war were to be declared, fighting would be initiated far from Shanghai. In fact, Clara had grown impatient with China's hesitance to take action against Japanese aggression in the north.

Shanghai, China
May 1937
Goodness, according to today's papers war seems inevitable. . . . If it comes to evacuation, I've announced my intention to wait until the last boat and miss that if at all possible. If there's going to be any excitement, I want to stick around, but I guess one is given no choice in the matter. I was informed in Singapore that China was one country where we Americans obey our Counsel and Ambassador. If I do have to leave, I hope Manila will have a job for me; I fell in love with that place in the few hours I spent there. Guess I fell pretty much in love with every bit of the grand globe that I had the fortune to see thus far, except Canton, and I'm even beginning to like Canton since they have begun agitating the government to give Japan the spanking she's looking for. (What the country needs is a Patrick Henry.) And I'd do well to stop right here or I will be receiving a letter or two from some Blue Triangle members who accuse me of being a militarist. What a life, but you must admit it's interesting.

By July, Clara was involved in raising money for a building at the YWCA in Hankow. A staff member there, Chi Yi Chen, sent Clara a letter on July 8, 1937, thanking her for her donation,

"the <u>first</u> of the sort." The letter also indicates that the Blue Triangle Club of Wausau had paid for a subscription to *The Woman's
Press*, a periodical published by the YWCA of the USA, which was
being delivered to the Hankow YWCA. Clara was smart about
fostering linkages. In August, she sent a letter to the Wausau Blue
Triangle Club soliciting funds for the Hankow building, saying, "I
have a sentimental urge of wanting to do something more exciting
with my benevolence allotment than drop it in the collection
plate Sundays."

Clara's activities at the Shanghai YWCA opened her eyes to
a world of differences.

> Shanghai, China
> July 26, 1937
> I'm trying to get up steam for the winter's program—if
> the war doesn't hit us first. Our "Keys" club insists on bi-
> monthly programs, and it fairly wears me out. As agitator,
> organizer and first president I feel the responsibility almost
> overwhelming at times.
>
> Oh, our club is loads of fun. One girl can't come to
> supper because she's an Arabian Jewess who cannot eat off
> of anything but certain dishes; therefore she comes later. We
> can't all do things together on Saturday afternoons because
> another girl is a Seventh Day Adventist. We have a mixture of
> races that makes me gasp, but you never saw a "sweller bunch
> of kids."

The war did hit them before winter. But threats from typhoons
momentarily overshadowed fears of bombing.

> 5 Avenue Petain
> Shanghai, China
> August 5, 1937
> Dear each and every one of you, individually and collectively.

. . . Oh, I must <u>not</u> forget my most thrilling news. We're
having typhoon weather and the other day got one of the
worst lashings in 10 years. (These are really ocean storms,
but they come close enough to go quite far inland before
they're spent.) I got off the tram Tuesday morning on the
Bund (comparable to Michigan Ave. for wind) and made the
sidewalk and the end of the block all right, keeping on my
feet by running—but on reaching the corner I was taken in
tow by the wind (and it was pouring rain, too), driven across
and down the street a hundred yards or so, and just before
smashing against a stone building tripped up on the curbing
and was slapped down on the stone pavement—receiving
an ugly deep, but small, gash in the left ankle, besides bruises
and scratches on leg, knee and hip. But it was exciting—and
think how my grandchildren's eyes will glow as I tell the tale
on windy nights. (I'll omit the pain which almost drove me
mad all afternoon.) I do wish I knew when to stop!
My best to all of you,
Clara H. Pagel

Her ankle injury was worse than she initially admitted, plagu-
ing her throughout the next several weeks. Treacherous times
were ahead, combining dangers of typhoon weather with threats
of war. For weeks, refugees from northern China, seeing signs
of military build-up, had been streaming into the foreign settlements. A sense of foreboding is conveyed in Clara's description in
Clara's next letter, which covers several incidents from the eventful days of August 13 and 14.

Shanghai, China
August 14, 1937
The stream of Chinese refugees flowing into the International
Settlement and French Concession is the most pathetic sight
I've ever seen—thousands of them, no place to go—sitting

anywhere—sleeping anywhere, in doorways and on
sidewalks, their few belongings tied in a bundle, a vague
stolid look on their faces—a sort of childlike, no, I would
almost say their expressions were those of a herd of sheep just
on the go, stopping now and then at anything that draws their
attention, sometimes laughing, sometimes joking, but mostly
just expressionless, just going on and on—thousands and
thousands of them. The streets are just jammed. It's bedlam!
That's been going on for almost two weeks.

The Bund, a waterfront area, served as the primary thorough-
fare into the sanctuary of the foreign settlements. The warship
Izumo was moored in the Huangpu River next to the Japanese
Consulate on the Bund; it served as Japan's base of naval opera-
tions and was a visible reminder of Japan's power. The American
Consulate was located nearby. Clara continues,

I've said in several letters that I'm in as safe a section in
Shanghai as I can possibly be. I was right. But that phrase
has taken on a different meaning. There is no safe place in
Shanghai. Never before has the International Settlement
or the French Concession been molested. But war is war, I
suppose, even though it isn't formally declared.
    Yesterday morning the rumor went around that air
fighting would commence sometime during the day. Shortly
after 10 o'clock I went to the bank to cash checks for the office
coolies. I was there but a short while when suddenly the
sky ripped open with a zoom, bang, boong, and a deafening
explosion that shook the earth. The bank was crowded, and
with one accord all the people, including the multitude of
Chinese clerks, ebbed like a huge wave toward the door—
except myself (because of my ankle) and our Chinese typist,

Dong Miao Kwan, who always accompanies me to the bank. He stayed beside me and said, "Don't be afraid, Miss Pagel."

I wasn't afraid—heavens, no! Only my heart threatened to pop out of my throat—where it had jumped at the first tearing crash—and my knees lost their dignity, and my hands shimmied shamelessly. I waited for the big pillars to sway— I even thought of Samson, but nothing further happened for a while.

So I relieved Dong, who immediately went to the door and brought back the usual wild rumors, while I tried to make my writing at least resemble my endorsement on the checks. A minute later one of the American bank clerks came to me to inform me that the office had called to find out if I had arrived safely. Then a few minutes later the office called again and requested that I stay at the bank until things cleared a little.

I finally got my money, the Chinese comprador (clerk to you) shook like a leaf while handing me the currency, and so did I while taking it. Had we been handling cream, it would have been butter by the time I slipped it into envelopes. Dong had arranged the trip to the bank for me with a private ricksha coolie, as the regular coolies are charging exorbitant fares these days. After the crash, I told Dong to pay him off and let him go back to our building, which was at a safer distance. When I got my cash, I naturally wanted to get back—quick. The street where the bank is located is extremely narrow— not even sidewalks, and at that, half is torn up to repair water pipes, I think, so we were pretty well trapped if hit.

Dong tried his best to get a ricksha, but no go; therefore, with the aid of his strong left arm, I walked it, about five blocks back, and that is the reason I am again forced to remain in bed today.

What happened was this: A Japanese gunboat is anchored in the river—has been for weeks—and three Chinese planes came suddenly out of a clear sky and tried to bomb it. That was some four or five blocks away from where I was. . . . The bombs came down—wide of their mark, two in the river and one on a wharf. Had they hit the boat, I doubt if I'd be here. The boat is said to be filled with powder and ammunition.

No further excitement, but I was glad to get home to the far side of the French Concession—the safe side. About 3 o'clock I heard more bombing. I was lying on my bed resting my ankle and reading but I hurriedly dressed and got outside, where a merry circus was holding forth with all the thrills of a war picture, plus the added thrill—if horror can be thrilling—of knowing that it was real. I don't know how many planes were in the air—clouds hid them most of the time, but we saw one grand display. We could tell which were Japanese planes by the pontoons. They fought all afternoon back and forth over our heads.

How lucky that Clara's ankle kept her off the streets! The afternoon of August 14, three bombs fell at the corner of Nanking Road and the Bund, and two bombs fell at Great World, an amusement park in the French Concession. In addition to refugees clogging the Bund, thousands of spectators had gathered to watch Chinese fighter planes targeting the *Izumo*, considering it a unique opportunity to view bombing at close range from a safe position. Clara's curiosity would certainly have put her in that crowd. However, the Chinese bombs missed their mark, instead hitting the Bund and also Great World, which was serving as a refugee camp. Twelve hundred people were killed and fourteen hundred injured, almost all of them Chinese. What possible explanation could there have been for the mass slaughter of civilians by their own country?

A firsthand account of the bombing, written by Mrs. Theodore Roosevelt Jr., was published in *The Saturday Evening Post* on October 30, 1937. (The writer's name was Eleanor, which has led to some misreporting that the first lady of the United States was in Shanghai at the time it was bombed.) This Eleanor Roosevelt sent a telegram to Madame Chiang Kai-shek, asking that further bombing be withheld until foreigners and noncombatants could be protected. Madame Chiang's response, sent to Roosevelt in care of the American Consul General, stated that the airplanes that had dropped the bombs had been hit by Japanese antiaircraft guns, injuring the pilots and damaging the bomb racks, which caused the bombs to "break loose." She said an investigation would follow and that an explicit order had been issued to prohibit bombing in the vicinity of the International Settlement. Roosevelt accepted that explanation.[4] The Chinese government was embarrassed, and the incident has had very little acknowledgment or examination. Christian Henriot, a French scholar, has studied photographs and what little evidence exists. He disputes the government's version of events, certain that the high winds and cloud cover associated with typhoons, along with inexperienced and unprepared pilots, caused the bombs to miss their targets.[5] In either case, it was a horrific incident.

Clara puts her situation into perspective in the next section of the August 14 letter, written before the major bombing took place. She downplays fear and clings to the adventure of it all.

I am all packed and ready to go. One suitcase had to be packed for emergency—in case of immediate evacuation—and I've crowded that to bursting. It's really awfully funny.

---

4. Eleanor Roosevelt, "Escape from Shanghai," *The Saturday Evening Post*, October 30, 1937, 62.
5. Henriot, "August 1937: War and Death En Masse of Civilians."

Shall I crowd my most prized possessions into this suitcase? If
I do, is there a possibility of losing it in the shuffle? Will I ever
see my trunk again? What about my precious scrapbooks?
And if I accidentally stop a bomb, why worry about anything?
Books! I shut my eyes and bid them farewell. My saris—my
beautiful blue and silver, and green and gold saris! But I may
be tickled to get out by the skin of my teeth.

While bombs were popping yesterday morning, I forgot
everything. For five wild minutes I had just one picture in
mind—Wausau. I don't think I ever saw it more vividly—I
felt it. But that was my first experience. Yesterday afternoon
I concluded that a movie of an air raid was much more fun
than the real thing.

I don't think I would have been such a coward yesterday
morning had I not had two weeks of steady pain in my ankle.
But I'm not bragging. Bombs at close range are terrifying,
especially if you're inside where the noise seems to surround
you.

I wouldn't give up my experience of these days for
anything, and I'm still of the intention to stick through. I may
change my mind after tonight when, we understand, some
major fighting is to take place all around us.

I could go on and on. I feel as though I'm sitting on a keg
of dynamite beside a bonfire, but it's just as interesting and
exciting as can be.

I'm wondering whether to report at the office in the
morning. It's dangerous down at the Bund. Did I say
"dangerous at the Bund"? The biggest casualty so far took
place about a ten minute ride away from the Bund in the
"safer" part of the city. What a life! In about an hour the guns
are supposed to open up.

I still think life is interesting.

Martial law was declared the evening of August 15. The American Consul General worked feverishly to arrange for evacuation of American citizens. The consulate insisted that the women in its employ set a good example, so Clara was instructed to prepare herself for evacuation, like it or not.

The American ship positioned to take US citizens to Manila had to be anchored twelve miles from the city. A truce was arranged so that a tender could come to the boarding wharf on the Huangpu River on August 17 to pick up passengers and deliver them to the mouth of the river, where the *Thomas Jefferson* waited.

Clara was in the first shipload of refugees, as was Roosevelt. The twelve-mile escape was harrowing, as described by Roosevelt:

> The tender looked very small to hold the stream of 410
> Americans, practically all women and children, that was going
> aboard. . . . Some United States Marines were on the tender,
> and an American flag was stretched in front of the funnel. The
> Marines ordered everyone to take cover. Quentin and I found
> ourselves in the tiny, overcrowded cabin, jammed in so that it
> was literally impossible to move. . . . As we left the jetty there
> was a burst of antiaircraft fire at a Chinese plane. For the first
> time I felt real terror. If a bomb had fallen near us, or a shell
> had hit us, we would have died liked rats in a trap. All the way
> down the river we heard firing, sometimes shells, sometimes
> snipers' bullets.[6]

Unlike Roosevelt, who was below deck and only heard the firing, Clara witnessed it from the deck.

Clara recounts her experience on the tender in a letter dated several days later:

---

6. Roosevelt, "Escape from Shanghai," 62.

August 23, 1937

I stayed as far out of the crowd as possible (but under shelter)
because I was so afraid somebody would bump my ankle,
which was swelling "swell." We had to go clear down the river
and out into open water to meet the big boat. And when we
got there, whew! A gale was blowing furiously. The tender
began to sway. When we had cleared Shanghai, we had been
allowed to go on top deck, and I went up for air, knowing
the inevitable sway in rough open water would make me
miserably seasick unless I could see the waves and the action
of the boat. Pretty soon the boat began to rock to a dangerous
angle; the benches, long heavy ones, began to slide to the rail;
the waves dashed up clear over the top, soaking us up there;
and then about four times the boat rolled to more than a 45
degree angle.

I hung on to an iron rod, part of the structure that holds
the awning and which now held a huge American flag, face
up. Why nobody slid overboard, I don't know. The lower deck
took water. Women and children screamed and vomited and
fainted. Some of the glass panes in the portholes were broken
by the waves. Oh, it was terrible! Finally they managed to get
the tender around to the sheltered side of the big boat. But
water was so rough, the captain thought he couldn't take us
on. And to top the climax, the wire rope holding that awning
support got caught in the ship's lower deck doorway and
ripped away, crashing down the awning supports at one end,
on top of people who were clinging to them.

I tell you, I just didn't "feel" anymore. My heart had
already dropped out of sight when we rolled, and when I
heard the command to turn back, I gave up caring. I simply
stopped thinking. One woman clutched the rail so hard that
her arms became temporarily paralyzed. She was quite crazed

with fear. I met her later when she was perfectly calm, and she said she had looked forward to that down-river trip for two days with dread and foreboding, and that she was just terrified.

After three hours, the tender successfully rendezvoused with the ship. But it was far too soon to breathe a sigh of relief.

A short rough make-shift gangplank was put from the upper deck rail to the door of the ship, and four sailors and officers literally hauled us over and in. I can't yet see how it was accomplished. The captain kept yelling frantically to us to hurry because he couldn't keep the ship steady. The wind kept increasing. One man who had watched our approach said he saw the tender's bottom four times and gave us up.

My leg was numb to the knee, but I was too numb emotionally to care. I wasn't miserable, and the whole experience interested me more than frightened me.

So I got on board and got something to eat. The ship was bedlam—overcrowded. People slept on cots and chairs on deck. Before I got to the purser's office to register for sleeping space, my ankle was in pretty bad shape, and I called at the doctor's office. The doctor gave the wound one look and exploded, "You should be in bed and off that foot this minute." He rushed to the office, found that nothing could be done by way of a berth or cabin, so he put me in the "women's ward" of the ship's hospital. I put quotation marks there: Imagine a double-decker berth in your pantry, plus overhead cabinets on two walls and a wire net "hammock" suspended from the ceiling holding crutches, leg, foot and arm supports—gruesome looking things—and you have the "women's ward."

I had one small porthole on the windy side that let in
enough water to thoroughly soak my coat that I had folded
up at my feet, lacking any other parking space. But at least I
had a comfortable bed, and as I was seasick most of the time,
privacy was a luxury—and I had a nurse (Filipino male)
to give me hot foot baths and my meals. The latter were
difficult to get due to the crowd and confusion. I slept almost
constantly.

Clara had survived storms and bombings and withstood injury and seasickness. She no doubt felt her ordeal was at an end
once she arrived in Manila. Instead, she was about to face another
danger.

5

Manila

After three days, on August 20, the *Thomas Jefferson* arrived in Manila. Clara summarized the previous weeks' events in the following diary entry, to which she later referred in a letter.

> I went forth on a tour of the world. I didn't ask for a rather heavy taste of oriental warfare; I didn't bargain for a one-round bout with a typhoon; I didn't look for a perilously close call to a watery grave when the tender that took us out to the big boat from Shanghai almost capsized several times; I didn't anticipate riding to Manila in the ship's hospital (because of my ankle) and being taken from ship to army hospital via stretcher and ambulance; and I certainly didn't count on an earthquake, the severest Manila has had since 1882, about a half hour after arriving at the hospital!

Yes, after surviving a typhoon, bombing, and a perilous evacuation, Clara experienced an earthquake. In the following letter, we see evidence of her unwillingness to succumb to helplessness or hopelessness.

Manila, Philippines

August 23, 1937

When we got to Manila, the doctor advised a hospital. Open wounds in the tropics are dangerous. So he had a stretcher brought on board (several women were taken off that way, one gave birth to a baby the second night out).

The trip to the Sternberg hospital was uneventful, except that I almost slid off the stretcher on the way up the steps.

I donned a hospital garment (because my bag was still on the boat), had my ankle examined, and lay me down with a deep sigh of ecstatic gratitude that I was again in the beloved tropics—palms just outside my window, balmy warm evening air—oh, just gushing over with happy satisfaction, when suddenly my bed began to bob up and down. For a fleeting second I thought I was at sea. Then the building swayed slightly and I heard a rushing as of high wind, so I thought it was just a small typhoon.

But then came a definite violent, prolonged rocking, creaking of timbers, things falling. Then the lights went out. A hospital maid (Filipino girl) came in. She hung over the foot end of my bed, clutching the rail with one hand and alternately holding her head and stomach with the other, moaning. "Oh-h-h-h, an earthquake ma'am! Oh, ooh, ooh!" I said, "Well, what do we do? Let's get outside and away from the building." She just kept moaning and said we couldn't because of falling glass. But all things end and so did this. The building is a large sprawled-out wooden structure—two or three stories—and it held. I understand one downtown building was wrecked.

A few minutes later, another prolonged rocking. A woman patient, hearing the second warning rush of wind, screamed for the nurse, frantic with fear.

I stood near the door ready to leap if things began sliding, or to aid other patients, if possible. After all, I'm not sick and my ankle has stood worse in the past week. A doctor came and said it was merely an earthquake; he'd been through many of them, although this one did happen to be a little severe (next day we read it was the worst since 1882). It did quite some damage, especially to the dock where passengers from Shanghai were still being unloaded. I was one of the first off the boat. The passengers were badly frightened, almost resulting in a stampede.

I don't know what my next move will be. First, I want my ankle to heal. Expect to leave the hospital for the Y hostel in a few days. I'm waiting for news from Shanghai, of course.

I've kept quite happy and interested through it all and haven't felt at all worried.

In reflecting on all she had endured during July and August, Clara was characteristically sanguine. The excerpt that follows, from a letter written several months later, provides considerable insight into her outlook. Prior to embarking on this trip around the world, Clara had felt an enormous responsibility for others, especially her mother. She was now experiencing a carefree attitude, perhaps for the first time in her life.

Dear Lydia:

I have gone through a lot, all right, but really was never badly hurt. No doubt I was in rather serious danger of being hit by shrapnel that one Saturday afternoon when the air-raid was going on overhead, and again when we left on the boat; and we were so close to drowning that there wasn't much fun in it. But after all, it was just as interesting as could be, and since there is no one dependent on me there was no reason for my

getting panicky. It's surprising how easy life in general is when
one can keep calm through the crises. After all, as one soldier
said to another who wanted to run, "Don't run, Buddy, the
bullets will get you where you ain't just as well as where
you are!"

Once Clara was released from the hospital, she was provided
with housing along with three other women who had also been
evacuated. They had been told that they would be returned to
Shanghai in sixty days, so Clara enjoyed a lull—she wasn't searching for a job, she wasn't looking for a place to live, she wasn't
wondering about where to go next, she wasn't even thinking too
much about the war because of the close relationship between
the United States and the Philippine Commonwealth.

In an excerpt from a letter to Bertha Pearson, Clara describes
what she loves about Manila. Bertha was much older than Clara,
but they worked in similar business enterprises, were both members of the Blue Triangle Club, and were in many ways kindred
spirits. Bertha worked for the Marathon Box Company for nearly
seventy years, beginning in 1909, and rose to an executive position within the company. She was an influential member of the
Wausau business community and a well-recognized environ-
mentalist. Clara and Bertha shared an adventurous attitude, and
the two of them took some road trips together. According to the
Wausau newspaper, the two drove to Yellowstone, Glacier, and
"other points of scenic attraction in the west" in July 1925.[1]

---

1. "Personals," *Wausau Daily News-Herald*, August 3, 1925. Bertha's niece,
   Suzanne Landes, sent the author pictures of a set of four hand-worked
   nesting tables from India that she inherited from Bertha. They had been
   a cherished gift from Clara.

Manila, P. I.
September 30, 1937
Dear Bertha:
You who takes such delight in the beauties of nature most
certainly should have a chance some time to spend a month
or two in Manila. You have never, never seen such gorgeous
sunsets. They spread all over the sky, and last very long. There
is a blue with a faint tinge of green that we never get in the
north—although it is not as breathtaking a shade as that
which I saw on the Bay of Bengal. The reds here are deeper
than I've seen anywhere. The clouds do such lovely things
to general effect, too—so many of them opaque white. The
grays make a symphony all by themselves. And then there
is the tropical moonlight. Nothing that any poet has ever
said can be enough to describe the moonlight nights here;
maybe the balmy air has something to do with it; maybe the
coconut palms have me going; I don't know, but I think I
could go sentimental over a telephone post in this country.
And how I love waking up in the morning dressing without
shivering; the same at night, turning on the cold shower and
not freezing to death; going out at any time of the day or
night without a coat—in fact going without anything would
be perfectly comfortable. Clothes here are nothing but things
to keep one busy washing every single night; they are quite
unnecessary. And this is winter! I am warned that summer is
quite warm, but not the intense glaring heat of Shanghai.

I love the way everybody lazes along; nobody is in a hurry.
Somebody seems to be strolling along all the time. Sunday
night is especially grand when everybody is strolling around
the big open space in front of our house; there is a band
concert at 6:30. In other words, I love Manila, and I want to
stick around.

I'm wondering very often what your reaction to the
undeclared war is. A small one sheet paper is published here,
"The Fookien Times," by a Chinese newspaper office. The
editorials are masterpieces. I cut out one about the move by
the US to bar shipment of munitions to either nation. I'm
having a somewhat difficult time holding up "our" head. The
three girls with whom I'm living have all been in China for
a number of years. They are desperately pro-Chinese and
inclined to knock the U.S. One is a Russian Jewess, married
last year to an American Marine, and at the time Ambassador
Johnson left Nanking when the Japanese warned all the
inhabitants that an air raid was coming, this girl said to me,
"Ha-ha, the Americans are losing plenty of face!" The tone
of voice, more than the words, made me go right through
the ceiling. I merely told her that the U.S. wasn't a country
where "face" was more important than "life" or the risk of
getting into a war just because an ambassador had lost his
life. This girl and one of the others could not understand
why the United States did not do more about the protesting
when hostilities first commenced. From this end everything
looks quite different. When you note the huge contracts for
material that China is handing out to Germany and Italy and
Great Britain (for railway equipment and bridges, especially)
you begin to wonder why the U.S. doesn't bid for the trade.
And one becomes rather acutely nationalistic. I haven't
been out long enough to go pro-Chinese; I doubt anyway if
anybody as completely sold on the "America-right-or-wrong"
idea as I am could be swung any other way. I'm all for Cordell
Hull[2] and any decision he makes I'm ready to back. Although

---

2. Cordell Hull, US Secretary of State from 1933 to 1944, received the
    Nobel Peace Prize in 1945 for his role in establishing the United Nations.

even at this minute he may be formulating a policy that will swing me over to the other side.

Clara weighed in on issues of the day, her opinions informed by newspapers, lectures, and discussions. She frequently acknowledged that what she read about the United States in what she called "'newspaper salve' out this way" caused her to doubt all news. But she also reported on what astrologists had to say. I don't think she put much stock in their predictions, but, as with everything else, she found them interesting. The letter to Bertha continues:

> I still maintain the world is an interesting place to live. At tiffin (dinner) the other day we met a girl who has studied astrology seriously. She told us some astounding things. She said it was impossible for Japan to come out ahead on this war; the stars of the Premier are all off. She also said that by 1938, one-third of the people now living would be dead, and by 1945 another one-third would be dead, so that by that time only ⅓ of the present people living would be alive. Also, that we think the Orient is where the trouble will all begin; we are wrong; it begins in Europe. She's a most interesting person; Australian; in the vaudeville game. She carries her astrology so far that she goes by the day and even by the hour with her personal chart. If the planets, say at 4:00, are not in her favor, she will not attempt to go out; she will wait until 5:00 or 6:00 before venturing!

Some of this particular astrologist's predictions proved to be fairly accurate. And although the percentage of the world population that died in World War II between 1940 and 1945 was 3 percent rather than 33 percent, it was nonetheless the deadliest war ever fought.

As her letter to Bertha draws to a close, Clara explains the appeal of traveling alone, which maximizes the opportunity to establish relationships with a variety of people, including people of different races and ethnicities:

This is indeed the country to meet interesting people, and so far it seems to me the people aren't nearly so "hard" as I found them in Shanghai. In the latter place the foreigners all seemed to want to be big frogs in a little pond, and it was hard to make any kind of an impression. Everybody was trying to be somebody big, and unless you had a title of some sort, or a stand-in with some official, you had a hard time to make the grade. I was fortunate to get a start with the YWCA, because even a "YWCA secretary" carried one farther than plain "stenographer." Once you got in, all was pretty clear sailing. Of course, I haven't met so many people here yet. That is the disadvantage of living with a group; you are too self sufficient. When I was traveling alone it was up to me to look around and meet other people. Now it isn't necessary.

... I am terribly fond of Filipinos: one here in the office has my heart going three ways from Sunday; the only thing that saves him (or me?) is the fact that he's about half my age, married, and the father of three children. He is positively adorable. The girls this noon intimated that they just simply have given me up. They are quite undecided what is going to become of me between the Chinese Mr. Dong and Parsee, Mr. Doodha at the Shanghai office, and the Filipino, Mr. Yan, here. Fortunately, all Orientals marry very young, so I don't think you-all need have any qualms of my falling for a single one and trying out an inter-racial hook-up. What a life! HOW I wish I could bring all my close friends over for a few weeks.

Further evidence of Clara's egalitarianism is contained in this excerpt from a letter to Clara Sodke, a friend who lived in Chicago:

> Manila, P.I.
> October 4, 1937
> When you wish to call a taxi, or bus, or carromata[3] or anything, the custom here is to "pss-s-s-t!" It's just too funny! You stand on the street waiting for a taxi to come along, and you hear these hisses all around you—Filipinos hailing carromatas. Americans do not ride the latter; I guess it would let down the prestige of the white man, or something to that effect.

Clara was certainly open to new experiences and took things in stride with an ironic attitude, so it surprises me when she frequently comments on the lack of "women's rights," by which she meant respect conveyed through gestures such as opening doors or giving up a seat on a bus. This attitude was prevalent at the time, but it seems inconsistent that Clara bristles when someone expresses surprise or concern about her being a single woman traveling alone and yet is offended by the lack of adherence to polite customs grounded in an assumption that women are weak. Here is one such encounter on a bus. It's clear that Clara studies people and sees their humanity—even with rooster feathers in her face—as the letter to Clara Sodke continues:

> Americans very seldom ride busses; I have been doing it quite frequently, but I never see any other Americans doing

---

3. A two-wheeled, horse-drawn vehicle.

it. Anyway, yesterday's ride was something of an interesting experiment. A colleague and I had taken a ferry to Cavite (ka-vee'-tee) just across the bay, and I got rather seasick so we decided to take a bus back. We were pretty far out and naturally the class of people riding were mostly small-village folk, with not enough education to "respect" women's rights, and especially American women's rights; so we had to stand up pretty much of the way since the bus was crowded. Finally, I got a chance to sit down right back of the driver. My knee bumped up against the back of his seat so hard that I almost got a cramp. But the climax was when a crowd boarded the bus after it was already filled to capacity, and one old Filipino had a cock under his arm. (Cock fighting is more or less of a national sport here.) The man tried sitting on the back of the driver's seat, using me as a prop. The cock under his arm was a restless bird and I was afraid I'd get pecked. But I hadn't long to worry when the gentleman shifted him, putting the tail right in my face. I didn't mind the tickling of the feathers so much, but you never can tell what may happen, so I finally lodged a protest and the man on the seat beside me, whom I couldn't possibly crowd any nearer the window, came to my rescue and told the owner of the cock that I objected. The dear old toothless man merely looked around and gave me a most indulgent chuckle, a truly sympathetic one, shifted the fowl an inch or two northeast, and we continued to ride.

Clara's tranquility was interrupted by yet another "episode." In this letter to Irma Gebhard, Clara again adopts a breezy style but admits to being frightened. It's heartwarming to read the reference to Mrs. Quaw. A major Wausau YWCA benefactor, Eva Quaw had donated her home to the YWCA. It was razed to make way for the building that now stands on the corner of Fifth and Grant. Giving Clara a pen to take on her trip encouraged Clara

to write letters back home and to write in a diary. Mrs. Quaw
no doubt saw Clara as the embodiment of all her hopes for the
YWCA: that it would enrich the intellectual and social development of a young woman who lacked many advantages.

Manila, P. I.

October 18, 1937

Dearest Irma:

What shall I call this—Episode Five? I think I shall begin
numbering them. Saturday evening I was robbed of about
130.00 pesos and the other contents of my purse—purse
and all!

There is a great deal of thievery and purse-snatching
going on in Manila. I was walking along Taft Avenue, one
of the main big avenues here, about seven o'clock. There
is a great deal of traffic on the street, but there just didn't
happen to be any pedestrians in sight at the time. I passed
the Normal School, in front of which is a lot of shrubbery,
and while passing one large plot of it I saw a shadow loom
up behind me. I thought nothing of it except that I clasped
my purse more tightly. But I hadn't more than done so when
I felt two hands on the purse, giving it a violent tug. I clung
tightly, but he gave another quick strong wrench and had it.
He turned and ran across the lawn toward the high fence, I
on the sidewalk after him, yelling for help. Just as he rounded
the corner of the building back of a big plot of shrubbery, a
car drew up and a Filipino and his wife came to me to lend
assistance if they could. They immediately took me to a
nearby police station and a secret service man accompanied
me back to the school. We searched the ground for about a
half hour without success, of course.

I don't mind the money so much, but I would like to get
my glasses back, and my fountain pen (that Mrs. Quaw gave

me), and my keys. My bag and trunk are locked and I'll have
to have both locks broken. I also had a safety deposit box key
and I'll have to have that box broken into.

I don't mind the incident very much; it's another
interesting experience as far as I'm concerned. But it's an
awful feeling to know for a fleeting minute you're in the
power of a criminal who will stop short of nothing. And
to feel that awful, violent wrench at something you are
carrying—well, it leaves one's knees rather weak about
an hour after. Without a doubt, if I had clung to my purse
successfully (it was straw and therefore somewhat slippery)
he would have either slugged or knifed me. The Filipinos
are noted for carrying knives. I have noticed a number of
more prosperous-looking ones carrying revolvers; now I
understand why. If I were a good shot, I'd buy one for myself.
Many people carry lead-filled leather walking sticks, or "billy-
clubs"; I saw a woman Sunday in broad daylight carrying
one. However, I still do not fear the natives, and I certainly
wouldn't want to try slugging one for fear he'd get me with a
bolo-knife sometime in the future.

WHAT is going to be the next episode in my life? The
astrologist told me that October would be a bad month for
me—but 1938 is going to be a perfectly grand year, so I'm just
holding my thumbs, wondering what the next two weeks of
October will bring. But between man and animal, I think I'd
prefer a rendezvous with an animal. I've had my try at the
elements, at man, and now I anticipate the animal kingdom—
unless the vegetable kingdom will come first in the way of
poisoning. My idea is to have a cheerful outlook on life.

～

When the war in China did not abate after sixty days, the US
consulate transferred its staff back home on an indefinite leave.

Not willing to cut her journey short, Clara resigned and began seeking a job in Manila. She didn't want war to interfere with what she referred to as her "ambition." That ambition was not simply to take a trip around the world; she was intent upon making her way in the world and stretching her mind. She was positioned to have a front-row seat for a war that reshaped the world, and she interacted with some of the players involved in that reshaping, including Kathleen Timolat McNutt and E. Stanley Jones.

Clara met McNutt, wife of Paul McNutt, the high commissioner to the Philippines, at a YWCA luncheon. It was speculated at the time that Kathleen McNutt might become first lady of the United States. Her husband had campaigned for the presidency in 1936. It is interesting to note that, while serving as high commissioner to the Philippines, he allowed thirteen hundred Jewish refugees to enter at a time when they could not legally enter the United States in large numbers. When the Federal Security Agency was created, he became its first administrator, managing an array of New Deal programs. The agency also served as a cover for the War Research Service, a secret program to develop chemical and biological weapons. Following Philippine independence on July 4, 1946, McNutt served as America's first ambassador to the islands.

When Clara was in Shanghai, she had interacted with Methodist Christian missionary and theologian E. Stanley Jones while he was staying in an adjacent room for a week. Based in India, he and Mahatma Gandhi had become friends. Jones's sympathies with the nationalist movement antagonized British authorities and kept him out of India during World War II. Looking back, Clara describes vociferously challenging his ideas.

November 3, 1937
As far as I'm concerned, Stanley Jones is over the dam.
About two days before the first bombing, he gathered

together a committee of church men and missionaries and put up a proposition to them that a cable be sent to Japan asking them to desist in their mad endeavor. Can you imagine Japan paying any attention to missionaries, when they detest them like poison? Then Jones was going to threaten them with a boycott by all the Christian nations and people of the world. What would that do to Christianity in Japan? Just how was he going to go about getting people to join in the boycott? How many businessmen who count Japan as their largest customer would sponsor a boycott? I asked him some of these questions, but it just slid over. I personally think he's very affected and almost childish in some of the things he does and says. He's very easy to talk to, however. I would say "spoiled" but not stuck up.

I wonder if Clara's opinion of Jones changed over the years. In the months prior to December 7, 1941, he was a constant confidant of Franklin D. Roosevelt and Japanese leaders trying to avert war. He was twice nominated for the Nobel Peace Prize. In 1963, he received the Gandhi Peace Award.

After pushing doorbells and utilizing connections, Clara eventually obtained a position as secretary with one of the largest law firms in Manila.

Manila
November 3, 1937
I LANDED A JOB!! I began to get worried because my job with the Government ended the 19th, and for almost two weeks I had been on the hunt. This substitute, a Filipino, tells me that this is the "most conspicuous" law firm in the Orient. They use queer adjectives once in a while. A great

deal of Spanish is spoken here and now I know I shall be
getting into it pronto. I just called a number over the phone
and gave it to the clerk in Spanish, which strangely enough,
he understood—dos, dos, ocho, dos, cinco, and he gave me
2-28-25 (that's the way numbers are listed in the telephone
directory, with the hyphens).

This job is what at home we would call stenographic, but
here it's secretarial. I may get my hand into a little court work,
and I may also be able to look in at the accounts. What it is
going to pay me I haven't the least idea. I have been taken on
for a month's trial. I am conceited enough to think I have a
permanent job.

Clara's confidence was well-founded. She sailed through the
probationary period and was elevated to a position of transcribing
court proceedings. Clara was pleased to later recount in a newspaper interview that her transcript of a particularly high-stakes
trial was accepted by the court as a substitute for the transcript
produced by the official court reporter.[4]

Often, Clara and her coworkers visited churches in Manila
during their two-hour lunch breaks, largely as a way to understand the culture. Her descriptions carry a dose of cynicism.

Two of us girls are interested in going to see every church—
and we have a rather good-sized job on our hands. In the
walled city alone, which is a small section of Manila, there
are seven, including one cathedral. Most of these buildings
date back to the 15th and 16th centuries. The walls are terribly
thick, and the churches are very large; every one seems to
have any number of chapels shooting off at the sides, with

---

4. "Miss Clara Pagel Returns from Trip around the World," *Wausau Daily
Record-Herald*, October 19, 1939.

monasteries and nunneries upstairs; always one or more
patios; and always, always, always old paintings along the
corridor walls, paintings with the queerest subjects and ideas.
I don't know how many saintly maidens I've seen on their
deathbeds, with some pious padres kneeling around them.
How these devoted males do adore the pale passion-less
virgin. I wonder who's kiddin' whom?

They also visited cemeteries. As the letter continues, we see
an example of Clara reconsidering her reaction to cultural traditions she initially viewed as humorous or baffling. In this case,
she comes to appreciate the comfort undoubtedly found in All
Souls' Day rituals:

The other noon three of us went out to visit cemeteries! We
took in three of them during the noon hour. (We get 2 hours
for lunch which usually takes us a half hour to eat, and instead
of going home for a snooze as most people do in the tropics,
we sally forth in the hot noon sun to do some more sight-
seeing.) The cemeteries here are regular museums of art.
Almost every grave has some sort of grand statue. The family
plots have really grand edifices—some miniature chapels—
a riot of clever and beautiful designing. Quite a number of
the graves have a bronze bust of the dear departed. The one
cemetery, "La Loma," is one of the busiest places I've ever
visited.

Hallowe'en in the Philippines, among the Catholics (I
guess 99.9% are Catholics), is one of the biggest fiesta days of
the year. The cemeteries here strike me as being the liveliest
places in Manila. The statuary, private chapels, mausoleums,
headstones are a riot of art—some perfectly grand. There
must be millions invested. Most of the bodies are not buried

in the ground but are put in large marble, would you say vaults or boxes, above the ground. Of course, these are of the millionaire class, and I understand this country is lousy with them. (Perhaps not exactly a million dollars, but at least pesos, with a little leeway.)

Well, the day after Hallowe'en—All Saints or Souls (I'm rather vague on Cathology and its Saintology)—is the big day at the cemetery, somewhat analogous to our Memorial Day. Everybody goes out the day before to decorate the graves, and by decorate, I refer to something far different than what we have at home. They use mostly artificial flowers of which mammoth wreaths are made. Most of the decorating is done in electric lights, creating beautiful effects on the statuary and in the chapels. There were thousands and thousands of lights. One Chinese chapel has a tiny formal garden in front, and stuck in the grass and bushes were large green bulbs, with blue ones to represent flowers. Imagine the effect on the pure white chapel at the back. The designs and architecture are so unusual and beautiful! And they use the very tall fat candles stuck in the ground all around the graves (of those who are buried) or propped around the vaults of the more wealthy. In one section, the poorer, where all are underground, there were countless of these tall candles. They give a rather big flame, and the effect was almost unbelievable. The cemetery to which I went is extremely large, and the graves are packed almost more closely than our graves on individual lots. Coffin must be tight up against coffin.

The strange part of all this is that those two days are considered feast days, especially the second day, the first being devoted to decorating mostly. As I understand it, the spirits are supposed to come back to earth that day. Many of the people take out a large picture of the deceased and set it up on the grave or in the chapel. They also bring food and drink, and there is rejoicing and serving and calling all day long. I am told that sometimes, suppose a child or other member of a family has very recently died, a big feast is prepared at the cemetery and everybody is merry, thinking the person is there to enjoy it all with them. At first it struck me as funny or even gruesome, but the more I think of it the more I think it is a rather fine idea. To believe in a certain communion with the spirit once a year must be a wonderful relief to sorrow. Just outside the cemetery was a side show and all the rest—bingo, fortune telling, regular county fair stuff. And ice cream, hot dog, candle, food stands about every 10 feet throughout the cemetery. It was just too funny for words to see the "Brown Derby" ice cream, hot dog truck backed up in front of those lovely white tombstones! The Chinese cemetery, which I am assured is owned only by the Chinese millionaires, almost defies description. The carving, the vases, hangings! (Many beautiful furnishings are also taken out on these days, even lace hangings. In several instances large canopies were put over the entire space of a family's plot—not a cheap canopy either, and the family seemed to be "receiving" in great style.) One of those nights the people stay all night and I am told that at daybreak a famous mass is celebrated. I wanted to do that but could find no one who would stay with me. Anyway, it just poured about 3 am. So I missed a soaking.

Throughout her life, Clara was determined to experience what had been denied her as a young woman, whether that was going to college or seeing the world. Once her father, who forbade her to attend church, died, Clara threw herself into church participation, singing in the choir, serving on the council, and teaching Sunday school. Clara dedicated a stained-glass window in what is now the Grace United Church of Christ on Third Avenue in Wausau to her mother. In Manila, Clara joined a church choir and taught Sunday school, just as she had in Wausau.

November 3, 1937
The Unity Church choir which I have joined is already at work on the Christmas music—meets an extra night a week for it. I can't imagine us getting started in October at home and the entire choir being agreeable to give up every Monday evening for it, besides the regular Thursday evening rehearsal. Of course, the same situation holds true here as throughout the East, i.e. dinner between 7 and 8, so there's all kinds of time to sit around from 5 to 7 or 8 and there certainly is nothing going on in Manila to take one out every night. The social life is not as brisk as in Shanghai. (But nowhere have I found it like at home, with our hundred and one meetings throughout the year, and our evening classes. There are plenty of evening classes here, but for Filipinos.)

I also have a regular Sunday School class now, a darling group of eight girls of about ten to twelve. We are at present gathering cans of milk for the lepers at Culion Island which will be sent to them for Christmas.

The Philippine island of Culion has been called the "Island of No Return." Once the site of the largest leprosarium in the world, it was literally a place of isolation from 1906 until the World Health Organization declared it leprosy-free in 2006. The small detail about her Sunday school class gathering cans of milk for the lepers touches me. Clara's empathy for those lepers was perhaps heightened because she, too, had sought hope in a dark and isolating condition. Clara's serving as a role model for girls of a particularly impressionable age, instilling in them a social consciousness, sheds light on what she wanted to accomplish with her life.

Clara's wide-ranging interests included stamp collecting, an interest she shared with Irma Gebhard's brother-in-law Roy Morgan Sr. Although that hobby was mentioned in only one letter—in the only letter I found addressed to Roy—it is significant because it might very well have sparked her interest in world travel. It was her influential boss at the box company, Guy Gooding, who introduced her to stamp collecting. In the letter, she confesses to Roy, "I did not think I would ever be quite foolish enough to get excited about stamps. Mr. Gooding was cockeyed, I thought, and I resolved never to get that way myself over nothing but a few fool stamps. But, omigosh, I'm sunk to the hilt now!" She tells Roy she has joined the amateur Stamp Collectors Club of the Philippines and, even though she's the only American member, is serving as secretary. She is also a member of the Army–Navy YMCA stamp club, which, she says, is composed of elderly men who are old-time collectors and who spend a lot of money on the hobby. Clara indicates that she's cataloging a four-thousand-stamp collection for a club member. She also benefits from the club's lectures and takes advantage of their library of stamp books, magazines, and catalogs. She thanks Roy for sending her US stamps, which she will share with the club, and she encloses some stamps for him, adding a handwritten note to the envelope: "Don't try to soak the paper off the backs of the Dutch Indies stamps—they fade in water!" He must have followed her advice; the envelopes containing Clara's letters that were given to me by his son all had the stamped corner cut out.

Clara's portable Remington typewriter
DAVID KEEFFE

Clara's well-traveled typewriter case
DAVID KEEFFE

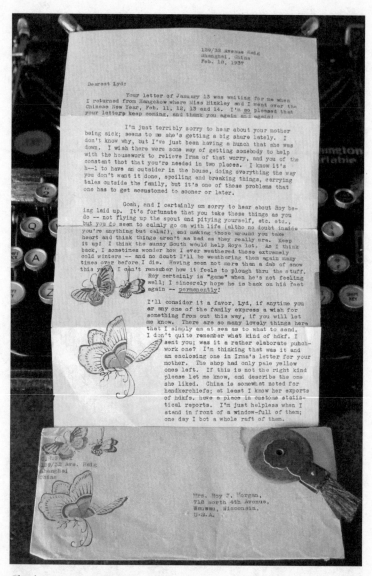

Clara's stationery
DAVID KEEFFE

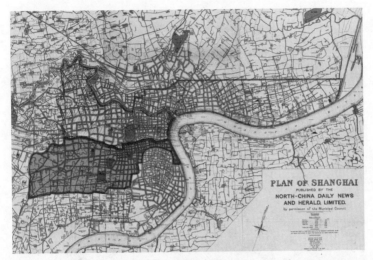

A map of Shanghai in 1928. The French Concession is marked by the irregular oval area in the bottom left quadrant.
LIBRARY OF CONGRESS

The Bund, 1930
WIKIMEDIA COMMONS

The YWCA hostel in Manila, where Clara stayed. Note the triangle logo.

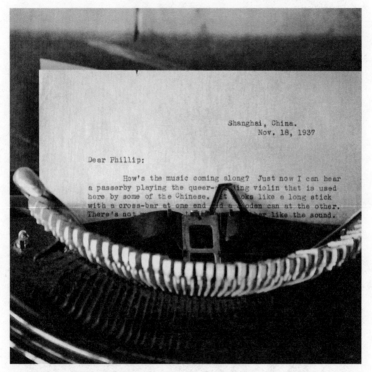

Letter to young Phillip "Bud" Morgan
DAVID KEEFFE

Clara (right) and Lelia Hinkley, 1939

Touring the pyramids, 1939
WAUSAU YWCA ARCHIVES; DONATED BY GORDON HACKBARTH

Miss Clara Pagel Returns From Trip Around the World

Keeping just one step ahead of trouble—and usually no more—Miss Clara Pagel returned last night from a three-year trip around the world, traveling by 21 different boats, by train and by air in the three troublesome years since she left Wausau.

Still unable to give any reason for her trip, Miss Pagel resigned her position with the Wisconsin Box company and on July 5, 1936, left Wausau in the company of Miss Erna Flatter, who at that time was returning to her mission field in China. Going by way of New York, the two boarded a ship for Europe, spending three weeks in Germany and Switzerland before Miss Flatter left for China and Miss Pagel continued to be fascinated by "how the other half lives."

Six Weeks In India

Six weeks in India were followed by some time spent in Burma, Malaya, Siam, Indo-China, China and the Philippine Islands, then back along the same route to Egypt, Palestine, Italy and France. Then this summer she hastily boarded a freighter going to Africa, stopping at 25 coast ports before the captain was ordered, the day European war broke out in September, to "lose his ship in the Atlantic."

This, followed by a northern trip to the Cape Verde and the Canary islands, was a prelude to the ocean voyage home on a small Italian freighter, headed for Montreal, Que., with no cargo and a stormy sea ahead.

When Miss Pagel arrived in Shang-

MISS CLARA PAGEL

after pushing doorbells and asking questions obtained a position as secretary with one of the largest law firms in Manila. Working for the firm, she became practically a court reporter because of the slight inefficiencies of the Filipino who was serving. The firm wished to have its own record because of the importance of the case, which involved several million dollars. Later, the court accepted Miss Pagel's record as the official record.

Remaining in Manila for more than a year Miss Pagel became interested in the work of the churches in the city and in the work of the YWCA. In recognition of her service, the Manila YWCA gave her a life

Syria she went to Athens, Greece, then spent two months traveling in Italy, later going to France.

From Nice, France, she hurried back to Genoa, Italy, to take an Italian freighter which was leaving for Africa. Because the ship made 25 stops on the way down the east coast she was able to visit in most of the countries bordering the Red sea and the Indian ocean.

Visited Dark Continent

Leaving the boat for the time she journeyed inland to Victoria Falls and Johannesburg, boarding the ship again at Capetown, South Africa.

While she was on the ship, which was at that time one day out of Nigeria, the captain received a message from the Italian government informing him that war had been declared and ordering him to "lose the ship in the Atlantic ocean for the time being," Miss Pagel said. She related that they traveled aimlessly over the ocean for a week before the ship was ordered to proceed to the Cape Verde islands and then to the Canary islands.

After she had booked passage on another freighter, which was bound for Rio de Janeiro, Miss Pagel was advised by the Argentine and Brazilian consuls that she should not attempt the trip but should return home. They told her, she said, they did not look with favor on "a woman traveling alone."

Boarded Freighter

Heeding their request, she obtained passage on a tiny Italian freighter which had been ordered to proceed to Montreal. Admitting that she had been seasick 80 per cent of the time she was on the boats, Miss Pagel said that the ship, which was without cargo bobbed its way across the Atlantic until it arrived in Montreal September 26.

The *Wausau Daily Record-Herald* hailed Clara's return, October 19, 1939.

WAUSAU DAILY RECORD-HERALD

Coast Guard Academy graduation photo, 1943
WAUSAU YWCA ARCHIVES

ISOLA

EN

HOTEL HOMANN

BANDOENG

JAVA

MONOPOL
MÉTROROLE

Grand
Café-Restaurant

Eau courante
Appartements avec salle de bain

LUCERNE

Près de la Gare
et Débarcadère

THE GRAND HOTEL

Cables-
GRAND.
CALCUTTA.

Telephone
CAL. 4709
(5 LINES)

CALCUTTA

ST. MORITZ

Bellevue au Lac

**HOTEL
SONNENHOF
MAINZ**

AM RHEIN

INH. OSKAR KERN

RAJDHANI HOTEL

BANGKOK·SIAM

Luggage stickers that Clara collected in the course of her travels

6

War and Uncertainty

The uncensored letter to Clara that follows, written by Lelia Hinkley, sheds light on the Japanese occupation of China in the middle of 1938. Lelia was transferred to the Peiping[1] YWCA in March 1937, but she and Clara remained in communication as best they could, given that mail was being censored and confiscated in China. That Clara was able to receive an uncensored letter emphasizes how skilled she was at networking. The letter was couriered by a Mrs. Miles, a businesswoman in Manila who went to Peiping to do some buying for her shop. Clara had arranged for Lelia to give a letter to Mrs. Miles; she also utilized an Anglican Mission as well as a business firm to deliver her letters to Lelia. Clara and Lelia, who had become fast friends in Shanghai, were planning to travel together during Lelia's furlough.

> Peiping Y.W.C.A.
> June 8, 1938
> Clara, my Beloved–
> Now that I know that I can write to you and say anything I please, I just don't know where to begin! Oh, it was good, good to have your letters.

---

1. Sometimes spelled Peking, now known as Beijing.

I'm ashamed I haven't written all these months. At first letters didn't get through and most of us stopped writing, and then when they did go through there was all this censoring and much delay. I still don't know how much our letters are tampered with when they do go out. There was a spell when all my letters came sealed tight with glue, envelope to letter inside and so on, but why, if they must censor the mail, they don't just stamp it censored and let it go at that instead of diabolically smearing them all over with glue and sealing them up as no letter ever was normally sealed!

Lelia goes on to describe the proliferation of Geisha houses and cabarets catering to the soldiers, whom she describes as young and confused. She also expresses concern for the injustice in property seizure before continuing the letter.

Fortunately, we have been able to go on without much disturbance. I've had my quota of visitors, but fewer lately. Somehow I've always been able to get rid of them without their getting inside to inspect! My worst tussle was with three pompous gentlemen who came to visit our classes. They carried "Department of Education" cards, but I told them in my most polite but most determined way that we did not allow visitors; that we were not organized as a school, not registered, classes were small, and our folks would be embarrassed by visitors. They finally left, but for a while I didn't know where I was coming out, and I rather expected some sort of a comeback, but time has gone on and they have never bothered us since. We're always having them coming in wanting to join classes, use our tea room, etc., but thus far we are quite immune within our own walls. The YMCA is overrun. Their dormitory is full and the secretaries tell me that they can have no meetings without a periphery

of "friendly visitors," so much so that most of their work is
affected. They have to be guarded every moment as to what
is said.

I want you to see Peiping, terribly—want you to come up
and be with me a while before I leave, and don't know what
to say. Peiping these days is a very different place from what
it used to be. One cannot go out to the beautiful temples in
the hill, and although the parks, the Temple of Heaven, etc.,
are still here, still it certainly destroys one's peace of mind
and any sense of worship to continually meet hordes of our
invaders.

My own plans have been so indefinite. I'm so grateful
you've stayed on and waited for me, more so than I can ever
tell you. Nothing will keep me from doing all the things we
have talked and planned about except lack of funds. It hasn't
been easy to save money because of the great needs all about
one. People have been generous and given me some money
especially to be used for the students. The YWCA has cared
for about 350 families for the winter and spring—almost 1,500
individuals. That gives you a bit of an idea what the need is
here, and yet we have had very little fighting comparatively
speaking. I dare not think what other places are like where
there has been protracted fighting and wholesale destruction.

Lelia, like Clara, saw the YWCA as a place where one could
find respite and stimulation. She mentions that a Business and
Professional Women's Club has been started, which reminds her
of the kind of activity about which Clara is enthusiastic. She then
turns to the plans she and Clara have made for traveling together:

As for the date of leaving—my furlough has been fixed for
the first of December. I was rather eager to get to India while

some of the conferences were going on. That probably can't
be, however I'd like to look in on the Missionary Conference.
Then there is the All India Women's Congress to which I've
been told I could go, and I'd love to look in on that—it would
give one a chance to meet outstanding Indian women leaders
of today.

I haven't begun to tell you a wee part of all there is to say.
But I must get this letter off, so I'll promise to try ordinary
mail again, though it will mean the soft pedal on many things.
I'm more tired than I ever was in my life before, but I look
well. One reason is that I sleep much more. I'm so exhausted
at night that I just roll into bed the minute activities are
over—no reading or writing. I even go to sleep over the radio.
I've had a larger one put in quite recently and now I hear
Manila clearly, but it makes me homesick or at least gives me
a queer sort of feeling for my one connection with Manila is
"you." The Japanese are careful that we don't hear much of
China news, even Hong Kong which was so clear for a while,
but now that there is the intensive bombing of Canton, it is
drowned out with cat calls, whistles, etc. It's so disgusting.
You'd think they owned the air as well as the earth!! . . .

Heaps and heaps of love. It won't be long until December.
Lelia

According to Nancy Boyd's *Emissaries*, about the YWCA's
work overseas, Lelia Hinkley served in China from 1920 to 1950.[2]
In the spring of 1943, Lelia was confined to an internment center.
One of her fellow inmates said that Lelia would be remembered
for her "skill in creating remarkably convincing facsimiles of cakes

2. Nancy Boyd, *Emissaries: The Overseas Work of the American YWCA
1895–1970* (New York: Woman's Press, 1986).

and pies from the skimpy and dreary supplies." In November, the camp was closed and Lelia returned to the United States until the war was over. She returned to China after the war and was one of the last five YWCA secretaries to remain there until the US embassy was closed in 1950, following the Communist takeover. It is easy to see why Clara and Lelia became fast friends—they had determination and fearlessness in common.[3]

In 1938, Clara spent her second Fourth of July outside the United States. In this letter, we learn a bit about Clara's health. She probably wouldn't freely discuss her health with anyone other than Irma.

Manila, P.I.

July 7, 1938

Irma, Mia:

I've been feeling somewhat punk lately—weak-kneed and giddy-headed. At first I feared another touch of dengue fever, but then suspected my friends the corpuscles. Sure enough, a blood test showed a rather startling deficiency in the hemoglobin, so I'm back on the Lextron—which I was swallowing up in Shanghai. I may even have to get shots in the arm if this doesn't do the trick quickly enough. Tropics

---

3. Lelia Hinkley graduated from the University of Colorado–Boulder in 1915. In 1971, she was awarded the George Norlin award, the highest honor bestowed by the UC–Boulder Alumni Association, for her "remarkable service in China." In 2009, she was featured in an exhibit at UC–Boulder, *Americans in a Changing China: 1920–2008*. This source indicates that she was interned by the Japanese for two and a half years. "Chinese Exhibit Features Revolution," *Coloradan Alumni Magazine*, Spring 2009.

just naturally thin the blood. Having been so far north all
my life, I'm having a harder time to adjust. I'm down to 102
pounds again.[4] I tell you, it's just no use. I go up; I come
down. I'm not going up anymore. 'sno use. I feel just as peppy
when I'm at 102 as I do at 112. Outside of this silly anemic
condition, I rate just about 100%. The doctor was surprised at
the healthy action of my heart when my blood is so low.

Fourth of July! Parade in the morning—glorious. McNutt
gave a grand address—which I read in the paper next day
rather than stand up in the awful damp heat of the morning.
In the evening (Oh—saw the "Goldwyn Follies" in the PM—
Charlie McCarthy, Ken Baker, etc.—swell) went down to the
Boulevard and gazed in awe and delight at the "pyrotechnic
display" and fireworks put on by the warships, the fleet
having come into the Bay a few days before, about 13 or 14
ships. They placed 26 very strong searchlights (shall I say into
the sky or air, or on the clouds?)—anyway, they "squirted"
them all over, and the effect was beautiful. There were
Bengal lights scattered here and there on the boats, too, and
skyrockets were shot off continuously. I was thrilled to pieces,
really. Funny thing—I often take a bath before dinner and
then slip on the housecoat over my birthday suit. I did that
Monday evening (4th) and then when we heard the fireworks
being set off and saw the searchlights shooting across the sky,
Joan suggested our running over to the Blvd., which is just a
short block away. I went just as I was, and was it ever nice and
cool sitting on the great big boulders that line the shore at the
edge of the Bay along the outer path of the shore-side of the
very long Blvd.

---

4. Pictures show that Clara was tall, and she was described as tall by people
   who knew her.

Clara continued to enjoy shopping. The pleasure she derived from it went beyond the merchandise to include the overall market atmosphere and the vendors themselves.

Thank you for the measurements. Since you are neutral more or less as to the color of costume, I'll just select whatever fabric strikes my fancy as I pass along the aisles of Yanco Market. These Eastern markets always hold a fascination for me. I love 'em—smells and all. They <u>are</u> so intensely interesting. You pass from hardware to dresses to fish to dress trimmings to cuspidors to jewelry to vegetables to livestock to beautifully beaded shoes to radios to baskets to pottery to knit goods to plants to cut flowers to etc., ad infinitum— with the odor of fish and questionable meat and sweating bodies and damp heat and dust pervading it all. I never know whether I'm most interested in the goods on display or in the people on both sides of the counters—or they in me. I could wander along for hours—but whoever is with me always pulls me up short in about ten minutes. Ho-hum.

Clara enjoyed a variety of leisure activities and was always eager to participate in anything that promised to be a new experience or that would awaken the senses. She worked diligently to establish rapport. Her letter to Irma continues:

Went to the races Sunday—Joan and I with Manuel Del Rosario, one of our junior Filipino lawyers. He's a race enthusiast. And, incidentally, one of the most adorable young men you ever want to meet. He's quite reticent and conservative (most all Filipinos are that way toward foreigners), and I've worked for months trying to break thru the reserve. I finally accomplished it, and is he charming.

I lost 9 pesos at the races but had a good time. If I'd bet

on the season's champion and he was in a two-length lead the last ⅛ mile, he'd stumble and fall just before his nose crossed the line and lose the race.

The President of the Islands—Quezon—has a birthday coming one of these days and it is celebrated like Roosevelt's, the proceeds going for charity—I think T.B. work. The grand ball is being held at Santa Ana Cabaret (the largest in the world, I'm told) and I'm fairly dying to go as I'm told that a dancing party attended largely by Filipinos is a veritable fairyland picture—with those lovely gauzy dresses.

While she was looking for both a job and a place to live, Clara first stayed in the YWCA hostel at a discounted rate of fifteen dollars per month in exchange for her YWCA work in the mornings. Anne Guthrie, the American advisory secretary who arrived at the Manila YWCA in 1934, described its building: "The sign of the YWCA blue and white triangle emerged from the trunk of a huge acacia, like the sign of some old English inn. It had a wide veranda with big wicker chairs, a book-lined library with a table made of one piece of Filipino wood that stretched the length of the room, an enclosed garden, bowling alleys, tennis courts, a gymnasium, and a swimming pool. Upstairs were rooms for forty-five girls opening off another veranda."[5] I can imagine Clara feeling very much at home there.

Clara made her mark on the YWCA in Manila, as she had in Shanghai. She participated in YWCA activities, emerging as a leader, and was recruited to be the auditor for their fundraising campaign. Within three months of her arrival in Manila, Clara was staying with Guthrie and volunteering at one of the YWCA service centers.

---

5. Boyd, *Emissaries*, 167.

Manila, P.I.

August 16, 1938

Tomorrow begins a series of lectures to the young business
girls of the YW at the downtown center. I have the honor of
opening the series with a talk on "The First Depression" and I
still haven't the least idea as to what to say, and no doubt will
have no more idea when I appear before the girls. The talk is
to be given at noon—about 40 min.

Clara began to think about where to go next, keeping in mind
political implications as well as the dangers she might face while
traveling near where the Sino-Japanese War was being fought.[6]

Manila, P.I.

August 16, 1938

Miss Guthrie is anxious to learn my plans—suggests that
I skip over to Japan before going to Peiping. It's only a day
and a half from Shanghai. Seems a shame to pass it up and
yet how I dislike to spend a cent in the country. Sometimes
I wish that I didn't have any convictions and that I could be
absolutely neutral and completely indifferent to any questions
of any kind. But no—I take sides and fight like the devil
and keep a healthy resentment long after the "sides" have
forgotten they even had any differences.

Manila, P.I.

October 14, 1938

I wish I could look ahead about two months. I am getting
more and more bewildered about what to do. The war in

---

6. The Second Sino-Japanese War was known in China as the War of Resistance against Japanese Aggression.

China has shifted to Canton, which is a very short way from
Hong Kong to which place I will have to go on the way to
Shanghai or Japan, and surely, traveling along the China
Coast up to Shanghai is going to be anything but safe. Japs
are Japs, and Chinese are Chinese. I think what I will have to
do is decide about an hour before a boat leaves and then hop
it at the last minute. Anyway, I am getting all set—Christmas
things out of the way—wardrobe somewhat in order—and
trunk contents decided upon. I don't want to lug my large
trunk back home. No more big pieces of luggage for me. I
always thot these wardrobe trunks so handy; yet, I've been
on the go more or less for two years and have never had a bit
of use for the trunk as a wardrobe, and right now my biggest
worry is to keep the mildew reasonably brushed out of it.
Mildew is an awful problem here and in China. It gathers on
anything and everything worse than hoarfrost at home—
regular long strings of it. My Bible covers I have to keep
brushing all the time. My leather purse is one mass of white,
and my leather traveling bag—oh my.

All I wish now is that somebody would come along and
kick me out of my "complacency." I just don't want to move
out of the easy existence that I'm in. But this will never carry
out my ambitions and I simply must break away sooner or
later. Will I soon be dodging bombs in Shanghai or shivering
in Japan or Korea or Peiping—or, right here in Manila
strolling along Dewey Blvd. in the balmy evenings—sort o'
drugged into laziness. Help!

At the end of 1938, Clara left Manila. Upon her departure, she
was honored with a lifetime membership in the YWCA of Manila.

7

Ceylon and Egypt

After a year and a half in Manila, Clara decided to continue her journey, though her route was complicated by the threat of all-out war. According to a newspaper account,

> From Manila she went to Bali, then to Java, then back to Malaya,[1] where she witnessed the coronation of a ruler of one of the smaller political divisions.... Capturing a bit of Kipling, she traveled in Burma, going up the Irrawaddy River in the side-wheeler, traveling as far as Mandalay.... In Rangoon,[2] despite the warnings of friends and the reluctance with which the guide took her, she visited the Shwe Dagon pagoda.[3]

From Rangoon, she traveled to India, where Lelia Hinkley, on furlough from her YWCA work, joined her in Madura for the international women's meetings. In the following letter, written from Ceylon,[4] Clara's reference to "respect for women" takes on

---

1. Malaysia.
2. Yangon.
3. "Miss Clara Pagel Returns from Trip around the World," *Wausau Daily Record-Herald*, October 19, 1939.
4. Sri Lanka.

a meaning that goes beyond her previously stated concerns about courteous deference:

THE HOTEL SUISSE
Kandy, Ceylon
March 10, 1939
At Madura the other day: We stayed at the Christian College—a Congregational mission project, I think—at the bungalow of a Dr. and Mrs. Flint, and the Mrs. a Madison product! They have been here some thirty years. When I say "bungalow," imagine a two-story home with huge rooms with all the comforts of home, and where the comforts are lacking there are enough servants to make up the deficiency. We were most cordially treated—really as guests and not as "paying guests." As chance would have it, there was a small gathering of YWCA workers that day and the day before— with one of the national secretaries (British) in attendance. The Y at Madura has no building and the way the women keep together and carry on work is most remarkable. Money is woefully lacking for the amount of work to be done in India. This poor British secretary was spreading herself so thin over such a large section—and she is such a peach of a hail-fellow-well-met type (so extremely different than all the other British women we have been meeting, even secretaries, that Lelia and I were plumb astonished)—I fear she is going to wear herself out—same with the Indian woman who is trying to stretch all over the south section. You see, America has withdrawn its financial help in India—had to do so in the depression—and gosh, India needs work among its women so badly. These Indian girls who are coming out in public life—nurses, teachers, etc.—simply don't know what it's all about. As in our schools, they are taught the fundamentals of their work, but nothing as to what they might expect at the

hands of a public that for centuries has been all male, which has had no respect for women other than they might be working assets in the fields or home. And some of the girls are sent way out beyond, alone, and lead a desperately lonely life. As Miss Taffs, the British secretary, said, "You simply can't blame them for going wrong; I'd do it myself!"

India has an awful problem. Gandhi is trying to raise the general scale of wages to 8 annas a day—around $.16. If I remember correctly, Quezon is trying to raise the scales to 1.25 or 1.50 pesos—62½ or 75 cents a day—and I thought <u>that</u> was small!! What a life!

I wonder if my last letter had enough postage. I'd weep if any of these India letters went astray. I'm much more interested in recording things now than I was two years ago; then it was generalities, now it's details.

Unfortunately, the letters from India either were never delivered or were lost in the intervening years. I did not locate any.

On this part of her journey, Clara was more of a tourist than she had been during the first two and half years of her trip. Her letters skillfully paint the various scenes in which she is immersed.

THE HOTEL SUISSE
Kandy, Ceylon
March 10, 1939
Here I am again, in this lovely, lovely country and in one of its prettiest spots. This morning we went out to the botanical gardens and while the memory is still fresh I'm going to jot down a few of the interesting points. Both of us were laden down with samples of everything.

Remember the cannon ball tree we saw in Chicago? There are four of them here, except that the one at Chicago was a sort of squatty thing, whereas these are tall trees—far taller

than our elms—and the balls grown on "twigs" that grow
out from the trunk from the ground up to the first branches,
perhaps some forty to fifty feet up. (Gosh and that may be ten
feet; as far as judging distances, I'm absolutely off.)

We saw one tree—Brazilian Mimosa—that looked for all
the world like a big fuzzy green tree with bunches of violets
all over it—a very tall tree, too, like our elm.

A guide took us through the orchid house and the
spice section. By the time he left us we had a nutmeg nut,
cinnamon twig, camphor leaf, pepper leaf, citronella grass,
bay-rum leaf, allspice leaf, a flower from the "Napoleon
crown" tree (red and yellow, looks like a crown perched on
a broad red cloth), and a "candle" or long bean-like yellow
affair from the candle tree, a very, very tiny "Chinese lime"
that simply oozes lime odor, a temple flower that spread its
fragrance over the whole car, a huge red spidery flower, a big
morning-glory affair that has a heavy fragrance—and just
now Lelia is trying to photograph it, you'd think I was "taking
poet's license"—so I'll pray that her picture will turn out
OK (and she is a darned good photographer—exceptionally
good—and has a very fine camera) and show it to you. Oh,
and there's a very "hairy" leaf—the leaf is green and the hairs
are purple so as you look at it from the side it looks like a
beautiful purple velvet leaf.

As I said before, and I repeat, I think these gardens are
the most beautiful in the world. The ones at Buitenzirg[5] are
perhaps as grand, but I don't think they contain as interesting
a collection, nor do they have the beauty of detail. If only I
had a little botany and Latin in my makeup. Dear, oh, dear,
how in the world am I going to get in all this study before I
die? History, geography, Latin, botany, geology—and after I

---

5. In Indonesia.

have it all in and am able to remember as much as I do of the
little I know now, it won't do me a bit of good, because all I
can retain wouldn't flood a dent in a thimble.

After traveling by train from India to Ceylon, Clara contrasts
the scenery, drought conditions, and cleanliness between the two
countries:

We are driving to Colombo this afternoon, some 75 miles.
By train—express train—it takes only three hours—but
we will be driving through what I think is some of the most
beautiful scenery in the world. When we came down the
other night from India we had to change trains for Kandy at
4:45 in the morning—and Lelia most disgustingly wondered
what gave me the idea of coming to Kandy. However, on the
next stretch, after the sun had come up and life seemed more
like living, and we were passing through the mountains—
no dust and all lovely tropical trees, with banana, rubber,
coconut, tea plantations going by, Lelia said, "I take it all
back; this is beautiful!" Last evening she simply gushed as
we walked around the lake and were rewarded by a grand
sunset. Kandy is nestled in hills, and homes are dotted all
over the hillsides—pretty, white bungalows or cottages,
almost entirely screened by surrounding foliage. The lake in
the middle is a pretty thing. And all is spotlessly clean. Ceylon
isn't India by any manner or means.

We had to report to the "provincial surgeon" yesterday
afternoon, and he was telling us about the drought in Ceylon
(which isn't half as bad as that which we had been noting all
through India) and said the Department was very worried
because the death rate is likely to mount. He had charts for
four or five years and showed us what happened during the
last drought. He said he had some 200 men out over two large

districts which he governs, putting oil on water pools. You
see, the rivers, large and small, run almost dry and leave pools
that breed mosquitos. Just as we were starting out for the
gardens yesterday afternoon, we went first to the provincial
surgeon's office, and while there it began to pour—poured so
hard you could hardly see across the street—the first rain in
two months! I think that is the second or third time we have
brought rain. We had to return to the hotel—and of course
had no sooner returned than the sky cleared and the evening
was grand.

Well! What I started out to tell you—(and there is a
water cart just below my window being drawn by two buffalo.
They have to make a hill and the poor things are balking. The
poor driver is beside himself and is yelling and prodding. I
don't see how they ever are going to make it, but no doubt
they have had to cover the same trail many times. Again,
what a life!)—what I started out to tell you was about a
dinner the women at Madura put on as a windup of the little
conference. We entered the dining room and found at the
long table a white cloth on which at each place (some 10
or 12 of us) was the top section of a banana leaf, or plantain
leaf, about 18" long, and the servants were placing the rice on
it, and at one edge a spoonful of an onion concoction and
pickle concoction. We all sat down and dug in with fingers.
There was no silverware—nothing on the table but a vase of
flowers. The Indian women would roll the rice in a ball and
then pop it into their mouths with the back of their thumb—
thoroughly sort of kneading it or mixing it with the onion and
pickle stuff sometimes. One woman at my right had greasy
hands and fingers almost to the wrists. (I was watching her
elbows!) They also served breaded chops which I nibbled
on all the way through. I did try some of the rice but didn't
"play" with it. Then a sort of fruit mixture was served in sauce

dishes and we were given a spoon. After that a small melon, something like our honeydew, was given us, and we ended up, of all things, with a bit of shredded vegetable or fruit— coconut and something else—wrapped in <u>betel</u> leaves! You've read of the awful betel nut chewing in India—makes the mouth and lips bright red—and all the sidewalks and streets, too, from the juice spitting. These were merely the leaves, which do the "red" work, but the juice is swallowed and is supposed to aid the digestion—same as our gum! In fact, one of the Indian women asked me regarding our gum why we chew it! Now, what would <u>you</u> answer? There simply ain't no rhyme or reason.

Lelia and Clara continued on to Egypt. In addition to describing pyramids and bazaars in the following letter, Clara reveals her far-ranging, quirky attachments and interests: automobiles, her typewriter, coffee, architecture, language, and fortune telling.

On the way to Luxor
About 10 o'clock at night
With at least 10 more hours to go and
no sleeping accommodations on this train
March 27, 1939
Dearest Irma:
I received your letter with the stockings enclosed, . . . forwarded to me from Colombo. I got no less than 14 letters here and didn't expect a single one! Some followed me from Calcutta and one from Singapore.

    And now for Egypt! I'm positively NUTS about the country! We just landed at Port Said in the morning and were met at the boat by a Maltese woman (not cat) who had been on the YWCA board. She said the Y hostel had been closed

for some little time and our letter asking for accommodations
had been turned over to her, so she thought it best to take
care of us personally and inform us of a good hotel. Then
she left and we proceeded to go through customs. A launch
took us from the boat around the shore to the customs house
a few blocks around a bend. We were told that customs in
Egypt were a bugbear and we would be in for one awful time.
When I took my typewriter, the American Express man said
we would have to make a deposit on it. Lelia got excited and
was all for shipping it on with our other bags to Marseilles.
I balked. (This little machine is just about my right hand by
now.) So we pushed off (as the British say). At the customs
house we went to the office for the typewriter clearance and
had absolutely not one bit of trouble or inconvenience. We
went over to the baggage inspection desk and explained
that we had nothing to declare; that we were merely tourists
passing thru and had sent most of our luggage on ahead; and
the man just asked that I open one bag, gave a quick glance
thru the contents, and marked all four of our bags OK and we
left—just like that! (So far we have been so fortunate that I'm
afraid we are going to head into something soon just to keep
the law of averages still a law of averages.)

We had to hang around the Express office almost an hour,
and when we learned that a train would leave for Cairo at
noon, we decided to hop it. The railroad follows the Suez
Canal for quite a distance and I was simply thrilled to pieces
watching the scenery and the life all along the way. Camels
by now have become as commonplace—or more so—than
horses at home. Saw a Beduoin squatting at one station and
my eyes almost popped out of my head.

Clara is astonished that the real Cairo bears little resemblance
to the Cairo of her imagination:

When we arrived at Cairo they popped further. Cairo is everything that I didn't expect it to be. Wide, straight streets; tall buildings all modern; big squares with statues and trees; the swellest looking cars that are made; as many Europeans on the streets as Egyptians—well, it might just as well be New York or London—except that you do meet up with camels carrying loads, donkey carts, women in black with covered faces (altho the covering is a large-meshed veil that does not hide the face very much), and almost all the men wear a fez.

After three days of wandering I am still looking for the narrow winding streets of the Cairo of story and movie. The trouble seems to be the ambition and energy of the last two kings. Why, we don't even hear the "baksheesh" cry of the beggar, which, according to all travel tales, dogged every footstep of the foreigner. Usually only small children will hold out their hands for baksheesh, then they seem to be doing it on the sly for fear somebody will pounce on them.

We landed late in the afternoon and after tea (oh, by all means TEA) we went for a walk to sort of get acclimated with the near neighborhood at least—along the street (long) with the grandest looking shops and automobile agencies (and, by the way, isn't the new Oldsmobile the stunningest thing you ever saw?) and regular skyscraper apartment houses, all new, and up to 16 stories high, and some even more. (I hazarded a guess that the law of averages is putting up all the buildings it can on this side of the Mediterranean in anticipation of blowing off the buildings over the half of Europe.) There is a grand shop not far from the Y on the order of Henrici's[6] and

---

6. This restaurant was a Chicago institution.

all of as large and all of as classy. We haven't had TEA there
yet, but we will—oh, yass, we will; this coffee is like drinking
excessively coffee-flavored mud—no kidding—and terribly
sweet. As I remarked once or twice before, when I walk into
the house, please rush to the kitchen to get the perk going
on an honest-to-gosh cup of coffee—again no kidding—and
serve me coffee a dozen times a day—and throw away any
tea there may be in the pantry; my nerves wouldn't stand the
sight of the label.

We have dinner at 8:15 (I never will get accustomed to
these ungodly dinner hours that run your dinner until after
nine o'clock, when it's time to go to bed) and breakfast at
7:30 and 8 (and who on a vacation wants to get up in time for
8 o'clock breakfast after staying up all hours of the night with
accounts and washing clothes and diaries AND FLEAS?).
More of the fleas later.

Clara and Lelia then embarked on a sightseeing tour to the
pyramids. Clara's description gives an early indication of her
annoyance with tour guides and related commercial vendors.
Nonetheless, Clara's smile couldn't be brighter in a photograph
of her astride a donkey in front of the pyramids.

We got home from the walk and had dinner and dithered
around until midnight. The next morning the poor "boy"
came up twice to call us for breakfast. Of course, Lelia was
ready; she always gets up around 7 or 7:30 and takes a bath
and is ready to go downstairs by the time I emerge from the
blankets and wonder what all the fuss is about. The evening
before the hostel secretary had told us we could join three
other American girls on a short tour to Memphis with the
Ramesses statues and some tombs and the oldest pyramid in

Egypt. We got started around 8:30. (We had met two of these
girls on the boat from Rangoon to Calcutta.)

So, on we went—to the first statue, where we began to
learn something about the hieroglyphics. There is one figure
that recurs time and again—looks like a bee—but the guide
informed us gravely that it was an ostrich! (You get the
darndest information from guides!) The girls swallowed one
bit—the guide told them a certain relief represented a row
of candles; it was a tabletop, the Egyptians not knowing the
knack of getting perspective in their pictures, as you know.
The girls were somewhat nettled when I expressed doubt and
still clung to the candle theory. We have since been definitely
informed that it is a tabletop and of course are crowing about
our super-intelligence.

We went into one tomb—Ti or Ptah, I forget which, of
course—(remember the "Almighty Ptah" of "Aida"?)—and
admired the walls with their exquisite relief work, and then
Lelia and I started on ahead for the next tomb. These are all
under the surface with rough board coverings over the tops
to keep the sand from sifting in. I'll bet there are any number
of these tombs hidden all over the place. No wonder the
Tutankamen discovery was hailed with such great fanfare.[7]

There were these tiny donkeys all over the place with their
owners trailing you all around trying to get you to hire them to
ride from tomb to tomb (walking in the sand is terribly tiring).
But my greatest find was a nice big fat scarab—black. I was all
excited and watched and watched him, while Lelia bargained
for oranges from a vendor. Then over to the next tomb where
we saw another scarab and squatted down and watched him
for a long time—and that's where we annexed the sand fleas!

---

7. Archaeologists discovered the tomb of King Tutankhamun (misspelled
   by Clara above) on November 26, 1922.

But we didn't know it then: we blissfully admired the tracks the scarab made in the sand as he walked—looks for all the world like featherstitching.

These tomb builders were clever as the dickens and every once in a while you are brought right smack up against the realization that the boys living 2,000, 4,000, or was it 6,000 years ago, knew a thing or two. Why, we saw some hinges on a folding bed from Tut's tomb that are exact duplicates of the hinges on our doors! I was amused at the design of one of the chariots in the museum; it looked for all the world like our latest automobile hoods—streamlined.

On the way over to the "step-pyramid," the oldest in Egypt, the donkey-driver one of the girls hired "just to experience a donkey ride" asked if he couldn't tell my fortune in the sand. He kept at me all the way. I had no change, but he was all for asking the girls to lend me enough. He asked me to come to where the sand was smooth, but we sat at the edge of a little rocky plateau. But no little thing like that bothered the driver; he walked a dozen yards or so away and came back with his "night-shirt" filled with sand and dumped it in front of me and proceeded to draw a circle and then a criss-cross through it, asking me to put in some silver. I refused but chose one of the points, and he began counting something or other and then said my fortune was neither good nor bad, but middling, but toward the end of the year it would "pile up." And I would shortly get what I was thinking of. Ever since I've been wondering what I am thinking of! About that time we decided it was getting late and I heard no more. I do want to get my fortune told at the big pyramid.

We came back by a road that led past the big pyramids and the sphinx. We had to look right sharp to see the latter and I was so surprised that I almost fell over. Looking from the roadway on which we were you see a great many

buildings of sorts—they are clustered very close to the
pyramids and sphinx, and the latter looks oh so small
amongst them all. Perhaps when we stand in front of it we
will get a different idea, but I always thought it was a healthy
size even beside the pyramids; and I always thought all three
stood way out in the middle of the desert miles and miles
away from anything else. However, a very fine paved highway
leads from Cairo almost to the foot of the pyramids and a
tram line runs all the way. A hotel is out there and many, many
other buildings. Now it may be that distances are deceiving
even at that short distance and I may find things pretty far
from the other objects after all, because I believe—no, I don't
know—but the Y has a camp just beyond the pyramids and it
is necessary to ride there from the tram line either by donkey
or camel or car. We are going out Friday afternoon to witness
some dervish dancing, and then again on Saturday to stay for
the weekend. I am eagerly looking forward to spending the
nights on the desert in tents although no doubt will freeze. It's
hot in the daytime but awfully cold at night.

It is an incredible coincidence that Clara encountered a vendor in Egypt whom she had met at the 1933 Chicago World's Fair.
That fact alone tells me that Clara engaged with people, but the
following entertaining description of bargaining also reveals her
delight at interacting with people the world over and her skill as a
storyteller. I'm glad Clara was on this train for such a long time—
it allowed her to tell a story, unconstrained. The letter continues:

The bazaars are breathtaking. I'm still going in circles.
The young shopkeeper from whom we bought just about
everything we got is an Egyptian who was at the Chicago
World's Fair in the glass-blower concession—remember?
Where I got warmed up? He said they made all expenses with

the 5 cent admission charge. This year he is going to New York.
I think this time with his silversmiths. He is charming and
quick on the comeback. Shopping in these Eastern bazaars is
more fun than a Dutch picnic, if you have oceans of time and
skies of patience. He never tells us the price until about half
an hour after you first ask it. First he says, "Oh, that's cheap,
very cheap—I give you half price." You ask again and he says,
"Never mind the price; I show you some more." You look at
a dozen or more of the same article and ask the price a third
time. He says, "Say, I have some Persian tea; wouldn't you
like some Persian tea? You know Persian tea is the best tea in
the world. You have some, yes? Chust to please me!" After
refusing him ten times, pleading that you are in a hurry to get
back to dinner, to meet an engagement, that it is getting late,
that you are tired—"But if you are tired then the tea will do
you good, yes? You will have some." With a sigh you say yes,
and along comes the tea—all thought of buying and selling
evidently having left the young man's mind completely. A boy
brings the tea (all these things spring up like rabbits out of
a magician's hat) and you find that despite the fact that you
hate tea, this Persian tea is like no tea you have ever tasted.
It's darned good. You finish the tea and wonder where to put
the tall thin beautifully shaped glasses, because the only tiny
counter in the place is heaped high with tooled leather purses,
brocades, silk embroidered garments, bags, rings, bracelets,
belts, leather "puffs," photograph albums—and more and
more piled on top of the stack every minute.

Then you finally come around to the subject at hand—
the price. So out he pulls a box of cigarettes. "Do you smoke,
my lady? Then try these amber cigarettes, yes?" You try
the cigarette—and how I love them! They are quite highly
perfumed and cost $2.50 for a box of 100 and they are rather
short and quite thin—smoke up in no time—but I still like

them. And so you go on smoking, and you feel that you ought to at least smoke half of it before you again revert to the disgusting subject of price, the shopkeeper meanwhile keeping one of his boys busy running back and forth to some place or other bringing more and more and more purses and puffs and silks—even after you have definitely decided on what you want. However, after some 10 or 15 minutes you think you've gotten chummy enough to say perhaps that the time has come when really the price should be divulged. And again he says, "Oh, very cheap—half price. Wait a minute." Out he scoots and comes back with a box of candy—a soft rubber candy smothered in powdered sugar—and urges you to kindly accept some as a favor to him. By this time your patience is nigh well exhausted and yet you don't exactly insult the man by demanding the price outright, although you do present to him a very sober face and seriously tell him that you simply must get home and must know the price. So he sobers down and does some mental figuring and looks up with a bright disarming grin and says, "What you like to pay?"

I tell you I just about died by this time! I said some silly thing like 10 cents perhaps for a $5 piece. He comes back bright as a dollar. "Oh make it half the price; why not?" And you realize that you are again just as far from the price as when you entered the shop, and you have to go all through the process of sobering down the conversation. Finally, just about the time that you are exhausted and he begins to see that you are tired—in fact offers, urges, pleads that you sit down—for the 77th time—out comes the price.

This isn't much exaggerated, really.

I was amused by an Egyptian the first day. I asked how it was possible for the shopkeepers here to learn so many languages; all of them seem to speak anything that comes

along—French, English, German, Italian—and he said by
listening to them as they come along. "Anyway," he says,
"there aren't many words to learn—only 'very cheap,' 'very
nice,' and 'half price.'"

Clara and Lelia are still on the train ("It's midnight now and
we have six or seven more hours to go") when we hear about the
fleas:

Poor Lelia is being bitten by our friend the flea. I began
scratching Saturday night and Lelia said I had flea bites. Next
night I scratched some more and bites of the night before
had turned a deep purple. Again she said they were flea bites
and she began helping me hunt thru my undies for the flea.
In a few minutes she began scratching and up came the welts.
They are awful. The itch is twice as bad as mosquito bites and
lasts for days. Lelia says she is unusually susceptible to fleas.
She says one of the girls at Peiping used to say she could see
the fleas jumping from the sheep onto Lelia whenever they
were hiking and passed sheep on the road. Anyway, Lelia left
me and began searching her own clothing, and suddenly let
out a whoop. But the flea got away. A cobra let loose couldn't
have caused more consternation. We didn't get the flea either,
and now Lelia is squirming and threatening to take off her
girdle preparatory to another siege of exploration. I have been
let off this evening but no telling. And when we go out to the
Y camp, we may have fleas in abundance. Pleasant prospect.
Oh, well, what's a flea more or less; I prefer them to the
bedbug anyway.

As the letter continues, we learn about Clara's frugality and
about the ways in which she had furthered her education. We also
see evidence of her boldness:

The museum! The museum! I never thought I'd rave about
one, but this Cairo one has me going in circles, squares,
and oblongs. Oh, I must tell you first about the passes. The
government grants permits or passes to schoolteachers and
educators in general. It saves you a lot of money, because
fees are charged everyplace you go. . . . Lelia anticipated no
difficulty, but I didn't know just what I'd do because we were
told they were very strict on granting passes—required proof
and even passports. So into the Secretariat we went. Lelia
showed a letter from the New York office testifying she was
a Y secretary. Fortunately, I had taken with me the credit
cards I got from Wisconsin U for my sociology study[8]—
and just on the spur of the moment I also took the credit
certificate that I received at the end of the week-long "Bible
Institute" that the Ministerial Association conducted back in
1927 at the Universalist Church. This was on "Principles of
Teaching." The fellow in the office, a most officious-looking
young Egyptian who seemingly loved to show authority, saw
the word "teaching" and said he would take that card as my
credentials. Then Lelia handed him her letter, and we waited
until the papers were taken to another room for confirmation.
Back he comes and says, "Miss Pagel, you get a permit, but
Miss Hinkley, I am afraid that we cannot grant you one."
Well! Here am I, a stenographer, never did any professional
teaching in my life and never expect to. Here is Lelia, who
has taught all her life and still teaches quite a few classes in
connection with her Y work. I get the pass; she doesn't. She

---

8. In 1933, the University of Wisconsin–Madison began holding classes
   in Wausau as part of its Extension services, and in 1934, the Extension
   contracted with the County Normal School to hold classes there. Clara
   may have begun to take some coursework when classes became available
   locally, an indication that she was interested in sociology study even
   though she was not pursuing a degree.

had a hard time hanging on to her temper and wasn't very successful. I was scared stiff she'd spill the beans. She was mad enough to chew nails, and the argument waxed, not exactly hot, but ready to burst into flames any minute. At long last the fellow noticed the director coming into his office and again went with her application to get his approval, and about 11:15 we walked out with passes for each of us. We have already saved $2 on museum fees.

Clara's descriptions of architecture are detailed. Once again, she refers to experiences she shared with Irma in Chicago.

We went to the "Citadel," the big fort-like structure on a hill, the highest point in Cairo, from which a good view of the city can be obtained, and where the old palace is (quite in ruins now) and also the grandest mosque in this city of mosques. The latter is the most beautiful mosque we have seen—it's positively gorgeous inside, with stained glass windows that catch the sunlight beautifully. There are thousands of crystal lamps and chandeliers. The place is huge; I judge some six stories high from floor to dome. The carpets are very thick; the walls are of alabaster, as are also the columns, of course.

The two minarets are 250 steps high, winding in a circle slightly worse than the ones leading up to the carillon at Chicago U chapel—remember? The Egyptian went up, but we desisted. (I would tell you his name, but I don't know how to spell it and the pronunciation requires tonsils that I haven't got. There is a great deal of the guttural "ch" in this Egyptian speech.)

We are in a "women's compartment"—one long, narrow leather-upholstered seat along one side and a blank wall along the other. We are traveling second class. I still don't feel sleepy, but wait until tomorrow—wow! Two or three days of intensive sight-seeing at Luxor and Thebes and another overnight ride back. A couple days at camp with the pyramids and sphinx to explore and on to Palestine and the trip to Jerusalem is a stiff one—also by night and very tedious. But more of that when we get there—if we ever do. Everybody advises us against it.

No doubt the advice against it made Clara all the more determined. She and Lelia did indeed enter Palestine before Lelia returned to China, while Clara continued on to Italy.

8

Italy

As Clara traveled alone throughout Italy from mid-April to late-June 1939, she took full advantage of opportunities to frequent museums, cathedrals, gardens, the opera, and the ballet—without passing up the fun of a casino.

Venice, Italy
May 2, 1939
Oh, before I forget—BEFORE I forget! The night at the Casino at the Lido turned out beautifully. I managed to get away with 35 lire ($1.75) to the good by playing roulette. But it was really my escort's maneuvering that did it. I had lost 100 lire, and he handed me one of his and said, "Just throw it on the table." I did and won; and then threw another and he just shoved it over the line to the left, and I won again. So I paid him back my "borrowings" and kept the 35. He insisted that I cash in so that I might walk out ahead. He was some 300 ahead and also cashed in. Later we went downstairs to drink and dance, and then he thought he'd like to make a little more. He lost to the tune of something like 600.

I watched a table of baccarat and saw one fellow pull in something like 15,000 to 20,000 lire in one scoop. The money

had been piling up and piling up in the center, and everybody
was getting tense. It was thrilling to see men put down 1000-
lire notes and 100-lire chips. When the thing ended up and
this fellow pulled in the whole pile, it didn't cause any more
of a stir than if he had been sitting at dinner and had been
passed the cream. He never moved a muscle—just slowly and
deliberately separated the chips and money and folded the
latter carefully and put it in his wallet, while his wife (I think
it was his wife) took the 100-lire chips to the cashier. Most of
the people around the baccarat tables radiated diamonds.

The place is huge and there are dozens of tables of various
games. I never saw money so lavishly spent. For some reason
or other it doesn't seem as bad laying 5-lire chips on a table as
it would laying down 25 cent or 50 cent pieces. I haven't gone
out again because I know I'd lose the 35 and a lot more. Now I
can brag to those grandchildren about the night grandmother
gambled at the Lido.

Clara's sardonic reference to being a grandmother is the second such reference she makes in her letters. Clara was happy
being a single woman, but she welcomed attention from men.
In referring to Enrico Celli, the man who accompanied her to
the casino, she says, "My escort proved very nice, but not a patch
on some of the other 'adventures' along the way. I don't suppose
anybody would feel excited after dropping 600-some lire."
The letter continues:

Venice is just about the most picturesque place on earth
as far as I know, and yet, queerly enough, it is a city that I
don't believe I would care to visit again. I'm too accustomed
to open spaces, and these narrow, narrow alleys and canals
and stone pavements everywhere are beginning to make me
feel pressed in on all sides. I shall be glad to get to a city of
automobiles and trams and grass and trees. I guess I would

liken it to a very beautifully-dressed doll I had received for
Christmas that just about thrilled me to pieces and made
me exuberantly happy for all of Christmas Day, but the next
day I would let it remain in its box and grab my skates and
go out for a good time; and I'd probably never play with the
doll, only bring it out for display now and again. I will always
remember beautiful Venice, but Cairo will be more alive in
my mind, or Agra, or Mandalay.

I see by the map that Vienna isn't very far north of Milan
and I am wondering if it wouldn't be a good idea for me to
skip up there for just a day or two—and then get caught
within the German border should war break, with half my
luggage at Florence and half at Marseilles, and perhaps
one bag at Milan because it would do away with customs
inspection going across borders. You know, distances in
Europe are so small that I look at a map and want to jump all
over the territory—and then I am stopped by customs and
visas. Crossing borders here is like pulling hen's teeth. And
traveling any place is a joke. I even had to show my passport
when I bought my entry card to the Casino the other night—
and so did Mr. Celli, in his own country!

Despite her reservations—and despite her frustration with
baggage—Clara headed for Milan, where the alliance between
the Nazis and Italy was about to be forged. On the train, she had
her first opportunity to converse with individuals who had been
directly affected by the Anschluss.

Milan, Italy
May 3, 1939
On the train today I was in a compartment with an elderly
German lady and two young women (German)—no,
Austrian, and two British girls. We had the most interesting
conversation. The two German young women would talk

the English surprisingly well, and they were such a lovely "home-y" sort. I asked how they were able to get out of "Greater Germany" with any money. They said they are allowed just 400 marks (that would be about $100 roughly, wouldn't it?) and they said they had put in their application for it months and months ago. Finally they got word that they could travel in Jugo-Slavia,[1] and they took the chance. They have to cross Italy, I believe, to get back home, and in some way (I didn't quite understand it and didn't want to be too insistent) they had only 10 marks to get across. And they take that sort of stuff and like it.

They said they were glad to belong to Germany; that 90% of the Austrians were. And I think they were sincere. They thought America a wonderful country—so free, so rich. England was also a grand country to live in. At least both countries had food enough. Germany, on the other hand, is so poor—so very poor; it is bankrupt. England is not. (I simply couldn't, absolutely couldn't resist the remark that if England paid America its war debt England would also be bankrupt. Sometimes I wish somebody would drop a brick on my head—honestly. I didn't say it in a snobby voice; just in a sort of sympathetic manner, if you know what I mean— and I hope you do, because I don't.)

Before arriving in Italy, Clara had been in Bombay when Gandhi passed through on a hunger strike, in Egypt when several Italians were apprehended before following through on their plot to dynamite a dam, and on a road in Palestine shortly before fifteen British soldiers were killed by a land mine next to that road.

---

1. Formerly Yugoslavia, now composed of six republics: Bosnia and Herze-govina, Croatia, Macedonia, Montenegro, Serbia (including the regions of Kosovo and Vojvodina), and Slovenia.

Is it any wonder, then, that Clara was in Italy when the Pact of Steel, the alliance between Italy and Nazi Germany, was signed on May 22, 1939?

In a letter written from Milan in early May, Clara says, "I'm still wondering why Goebbels and Goehring were traveling around the Near East last month; I'm wondering plenty why this boy Ribbentrop (may he have lumps in his mashed potatoes!) has come for consultation with Ciano, the Foreign Minister of Italy." By referring to the German Foreign Minister as "boy," her attitude is clear, but she seems oblivious to the foreboding of his arrival in Milan. Given what we know, her description of the scene is chilling, from flags to swastikas, from the uniforms of baggy knickers (plus-fours) with leg wraps (puttees) to the blackshirts of the Italian Fascist party.

Milan, Italy

May 7, 1939

Yesterday morning I heard bands and companies marching past. I hurried downstairs and learned that Ribbentrop was passing thru on his way to Lake Como at eleven o'clock. Uniformed individuals were lined up elbow to elbow as far as I could see both ways—young boys in olive-drab plus-fours with white puttees; boys, younger, in blue and grey boy-scout attire; another company of boys in blue sailor suits; soldiers with all the many kinds of uniforms; blackshirts; and just civilians who also joined the columns and marched; there were also several groups of girls in black and white uniforms—older girls and very young girls. There were any number of bands. Well, I stood down there from about ten o'clock until shortly after eleven. And then I decided to run up to my room (3rd floor) and watch the show from there, and just then the boy passed—I almost missed him entirely; as it was, I saw just a glimpse of him. There followed at least a hundred cars, all with officers of some sort or another in them. And all that fuss for the one car holding Ribbentrop. Women threw flowers from balconies—and you should see the flags displayed from all the buildings—German and Italian—huge ones. All these business houses must have a supply of the swastika. As soon as the cars passed, the mobs dispersed.

This afternoon around four o'clock, the same sort of fuss started; band after band and company after company marching past to the Piazza La Scala—just a short block from here. I followed and stood around for almost an hour when finally a door in a balcony on the government building opened and there again was this boy Ribbentrop! I could have shot myself for having stood there all that time! Anyway, I did hear some good band music. For most of the hour the different bands were keeping up a sort of impromptu band concert.

What interested me is that it seems the same people took part in this affair as those of yesterday. And I noticed that the "marchers" were all gathered in the center of the square or piazza, while the "all and sundry" were standing around the edges on the sidewalks. When the big boy came out, those in the piazza cheered wildly and loudly, while the general crowd around the edges merely looked on. I was amused on glancing back, as I pushed off, to see that when Ribbentrop turned to walk inside, an Italian officer leaned over the balcony and motioned to the crowd below to "whoop her up" even more loudly. That made me wonder if all this fuss isn't a put-up show. After all, why should the ordinary man of any nation become wildly excited about a mere foreign minister of another nation—excited to the point where they will hold their flags and banners and guns high in the air and throw up their hats? I've been thinking a lot since this afternoon and going back over many conversations I have had the past two weeks. I've just got to be careful when I finally put my 2 and 2 together that I get 4 instead of 22. Anyway, it is all extremely interesting.

In the same letter, Clara quotes from a May 4 diary entry in which she described a conversation she had with the travel agent. (Clara was utilizing the services of the Thomas Cook & Son Travel Agency, which launched a system in Italy to facilitate tourism by issuing railway tickets and coupons that could be used for lodging and meals.)

He also said that we couldn't compare or treat in the same way a country like America or England with their modern trend of thought as we would a country like Italy which is old, has old ideas, old traditions, old customs, old habits, old "thought." And I suddenly began to see his point. I began to wonder if, after all, Mussolini isn't more capable of running Italy and the Italians than is the League of Nations—or the fellows who write our newspaper headlines! If only our legislators could spend a few months in every important country before they do any legislating or express any opinions about that country. I have been here only a couple weeks, but I have most certainly felt that Italy is the most peaceful country that I've struck since January. The Dutch Indies are afraid of Japan; all the British countries are scared stiff that war will break any minute, and you can feel it as you travel thru; Burma was filled with riots and rebellion; India was all up in the air between themselves; Egypt was getting all hot and bothered about Italy coming in; Palestine of course was an awful mess; Syria was calling men to the colors, also scared that Italy had her next on the list (how they hate the Italians!)—and here everything is as peaceful as the lake district of our beloved Wisconsin. I'm sure I don't know what it is all about. I'm trying hard to find out.

❧

Clara visited cathedrals throughout her trip, although she admitted that "what I know about the cathedrals of Europe wouldn't fill a mustard seed. Let me see—St. Peter's at Rome; Santa Maria del Fiore at Florence, St. Mark's in Venice, and the one at Cologne or Koln, Germany. By the time I reach home they will all be one grand jumble in my memory, no doubt." In the May 7 letter, Clara relates an amusing anecdote about her encounter with elevator operators at the Cathedral in Milan.

I bought a ticket to go on the elevator to the roof of the Cathedral. When the old man sold me the ticket, he motioned me to the elevator and then got in himself to take me up, but first he asked me for my ticket! He solemnly tore it in half and handed me half. Then he took me up. When I rang for the elevator to go down, a young man answered and insisted I present the other half of that ticket before he'd let me in the elevator! I wondered how in Hades they figured that anybody would be coming down on the elevator who hadn't bought a round-trip ticket in the first place! Funny things happen in this hemisphere.

She goes on to describe the cathedral:

My, it's breathtaking. The huge main front doors are bronze done in relief some 6" deep. The bronze, of course, is weathered to black green—except in the lower right hand corner the Christ child in a cradle is highly polished and gleams like a light. It keeps in that condition by people constantly touching it and then making the sign of the cross—reminding me of the foot of the statue of St. Peter at St. Peter's Cathedral, Rome, which has been actually worn down by touches and kisses! The Catholic religion is indeed a demonstrative one, to say the least.

She concludes that the cathedral "is positively the most beautiful thing I've ever seen in the way of buildings. (Now, don't bring up the Taj Mahal. That's tucked away in an alabaster box in one corner of my mind and just doesn't enter the picture when I speak of any other place.)"

Clara's letters, especially from Italy, make us feel as if we're with her as she describes the settings and the performances in which she is indulging. She is, in fact, taking Blue Triangle members on a trip around the world through her letters. She worries that, once she returns, she may make a bore of herself, saying, "I never did like to listen to the other fellow tell about his travels, and I'm terribly sensitive about it now as regards myself. Should I see one yawn or straying eye, I shall shut up like a clam."

Milan, Italy
May 7, 1939
Saturday night I went to the symphony concert at the LaScala; I was surprised at the smallness of the place, given that it is one of the world's famous opera houses. There was a curtain in front of the stage so I couldn't see how large that was, but as the men went through and parted the curtain, what I could see seemed to be spacious and very high; in fact, it reaches clear to the ceiling. There is no balcony or gallery, but there are boxes built all around right up to the ceiling— very tiny boxes. The royal box is in the rear—and the rear is such a short distance from the front. All seats are red plush. Ushers are in knee-breeches and wear heavy gold chains around their shoulders with a large medallion in front. (This

country does love costumes and uniforms. Even I am getting
accustomed to them and no longer stare.)

Reminding me: Stare. I think the main pastime in the
theatre is staring point-blank and for minutes at a time at
anybody and everybody thru opera glasses and lorgnettes. By
the time the evening ended I wanted to shoot a few people.
They are merciless! They quite deliberately look you right in
the eye and then pass up and down you—just as tho you were
one more exhibit in an insectarium—and then they pass on
to the next one. The men are as bad as the women—only they
use the one goggle (monocle). Women seem to love the idea
of putting their glasses up to their eyes and staring around;
it gives them something to do with one hand, anyway. I
noticed one woman in front of me whose glasses were so
thick that I'm sure she can barely see without them, but she
merely uses them to stare around. She gave me the once-over
a couple times, deliberately turned right around and studied
me carefully. I trust she recognized the species and liked the
specimen.

Not all performances Clara attended were high-brow, however. Invited by a male escort to attend the theater, she worried
that she wouldn't understand a word. She writes,

But I was quite mistaken. True, I didn't understand any
words, but it was a sort of Variety-Follies affair and one
didn't need to understand to enjoy it. Of course, there were
one or two acts in which the jokes were the thing, but the
gestures, etc., of the artists were so clever that I even enjoyed
them. One fellow put on the old act of imitating important
personages, but his portrayal of Greta Garbo was just too
funny for words. The audience just howled—and so did I,
even tho I didn't know what he was actually saying. I <u>know</u>

what he was saying when he pulled off the usual, "I want to be alone."

The crowning event was an American quartet—four fellows singing like different instruments. These boys sang English, although one song was in Italian, which they no doubt memorized since coming to Italy. When they came on to the stage a wave of applause went over the audience; and they were encored four or five times.

Clara's stay in a pensione in Florence afforded her an opportunity to increase her knowledge and further expand her worldview through interaction with people from a variety of backgrounds. Her letters are filled with descriptions of people and conversations. Her fascination with Mrs. Wasilko, a fellow pensione guest, is clear in the following letter:

Florence, Italy
May 15, 1939
First I must tell you of the New York girl. She is a baroness—comes from a well-to-do family of Austria. At 21 she went to America, her father suggesting that she look the country over—a sort of gift from him. He died meanwhile and she realized she was without funds because their properties were in such a state that nothing was left after the smoke cleared. So she decided to stay in America and work. Her mother and near relatives were horrified—a "baroness" working—with her hands—accepting money—handling money!! She says it took years for them to get over the shock. She finally took out citizenship papers. She is now 39 and a divorcee. Her work in America these last years seems to have been—as far as I can decipher without becoming too curious about details—taking pictures for ads for "Vogue" and some of the other fashion magazines. She speaks of clearing $1,200 a month,

and of the magnificent apartment and penthouse and studio
she shares with a business partner, and of traveling back and
forth to Europe on business every year, all expenses paid,
and first class everything. She brought her car over once, and
casually remarks about it costing $500 or $600 to do so, just
as I would remark that I sent a cable or airmail letter. Royalty
seemingly means a lot on this continent, and no doubt with
her title she had an "in" where we commoners would never be
able to go.

I'd give a lot to have her education. She was in a convent
eight years and I gather those places are pretty strict, resulting
in some rather keen minds filled with just about everything.
She can gush forth history and art and music until I blush
with shame at my meagre fund of knowledge along those
lines. Of course, she has grown up with most of it. She tosses
about the names and titles of European nobility like a juggler
tosses balls—and just as easily and lightly—and always with
a sincere respect. She's a tiny thing, and speaks very broken
English, but she's ambitious, although she has the disposition
that will give up $1,200 a month net income with all the
luxury of a New York penthouse and loads of travel for $125
a month trust income and a small room in an inexpensive
pensione with all the inconveniences that a European
pensione necessarily means—no hot running water, no steam
heat, stone floors without rugs, plain (but wholesome) food,
etc., etc. But she gets inspiration and can enjoy nature—"and
these things which are ancient—which were alive when
America was not yet born—which will still be here when
America has died!" She is learning bookbinding while in
Florence—just to have something to do. Her partner got
married and they gave up the business. She came to Europe
for a year or so to absorb atmosphere and rest and to let her
partner and the husband get adjusted to each other, because

they insist she live with them and she didn't want to do so
immediately. Then she expects to hibernate in Connecticut,
living on her $125 per month income and binding the books
of the Gold Coasters to make money on the side. And I'll bet
she'll be a howling success, because I'm sure she knows most
of the "uppers" for whom she can bind old, old books and
charge plenty.

I give you all this background because my letters no
doubt will be filled with references to her—Mrs. Wasilko
(W pronounced as V), which is her maiden name, but she
hangs onto the "Mrs." cuz she says "it gets away with murder,"
whatever that might mean. She is not so clear on the English
language and sometimes expresses herself in a most amazing
way. She's one peach to me. She said when she heard that a
real honest-to-goodness American was coming to this house
she was so glad she wanted to dance. She's pretty homesick
for Connecticut. So I have been getting loads of attention
from her and she has acted as my guide day after day. She will
haul me to one side as we walk down the street and make
me look up at some old building (they are all old, but some
are older) and then begin to explain about the window, the
iron doodads hanging around it, the political leanings of the
owner expressed by the architecture, etc. And then she'll
grab my arm and say, "Have you seen Dante's house? Come,
I show you. It's not much to see, but your friends will ask
you have you seen it. Now I show it to you. It's just a little
ways—well, come along!" And off in the other direction we
will go. She may want to get to some place, but there is always
time to drag me around another corner. Needless to say, I
am delighted! She was here about three months last year and
is now here again for over a month, so she knows the place
inside out, besides knowing all the history of Italy in general.

One evening Mrs. Wasilko got started on international

politics. She, being an Austrian by birth and up-bringing, resents with all her might the recent "Anschluss" of course. I wish you could have heard her talking to the German girl! No sparks flying, but there was intensity in her manner that made all the other girls and the Dutch woman sit as tho dumbfounded or spellbound. I never heard such oratory. As I learn to know her better I realize she loves to hold forth on almost anything. It is she who is usually talking at the table, from the soup to the cheese-fruit-nuts.

The German girl got rather angry here and there and tried to put in an oar, but no go. When it was finished—and it went on fully an hour—Mrs. W. got up, shook hands, and we went out for a walk—just like that! I thanked my lucky stars that time that I understood the German.

Clara attended several performances during the Firenze Maggio (Florence May Festival), and it becomes clear that she was no stranger to classical music, opera, or ballet. She evidently traveled frequently to Chicago, which today is a four-hour drive from Wausau, to attend various performances. In her lead-up to describing her experience of *Il trovatore*, she mentions that Rachmaninoff was to perform but didn't. She also talks about the crush of people lined up by six o'clock in the evening for the nine o'clock opera and complains that, when the doors opened at seven thirty, everybody tried to get through at once: "One young boy pushed me so hard that I expected to land somewhere beyond Egypt, except that the woman in front of me was halted by somebody in front of her who was halted by—ad infinitum. Finally, just as I thought either a rib must bust or I must stop breathing, I twisted as much as I could in the press and told him to, for goodness sake, go up ahead—and he did! There's no such thing in this country as women first—not on your life!"

Florence, Italy
May 16, 1939
Friday night (May 12) was one of these unforgettable ones.
"Il Trovatore" was being played. The opera was perfect, of
course. All of the scenes but one were extremely dim. In the
last scene Leonora was in black and all we could see was her
face and hands. The lovely thing about seeing an opera here
is that it seems so natural. You have just come into the opera
house from a narrow stone-paved street, lined with stone
houses and the policemen and soldiers are in bright uniforms
and there are flags all over of every description—and you step
into a theatre to see an opera with a stage setting completely
in harmony with the things around you every day. And when
you leave the theatre, instead of coming out into the glaring
rush of a big city like in Chicago, with taxis rushing and
honking like mad and everybody in a hurry to get to the next
place, you walk out leisurely and find very few or no taxis or
cars, and everybody seemingly standing around or walking
off as though they had all night—no noise, no hustling—with
all the flags, and stone pavements, and stone houses, and
uniforms along the way to help you keep that atmosphere of
the opera right with you thru the night.

Sunday night Mrs. W. and I went to Verdi's "Requiem"
in one of the largest and oldest churches here. It was most
impressive—the high stone church, the gorgeous altar,
the priceless frescoes all around, the equally priceless
painted windows, the old-old-oldness of the whole thing,
the massiveness of the whole structure—or I should say
immensity of the interior. (And which was almost most
impressive—at least physically—was the intense clammy
coldness of the place. This remark sandwiched in to bring
you to earth. That's the trouble with this country—some

darned thing to make you take a headlong plunge from the
sublime to the ridiculous every once in a while.) It was quite
some experience. The churches do not have pews here as we
have at home. There are a few plain wooden benches with
the "kneeling board," but most of the floor space is empty,
and then you can "rent" a small chair and go and sit in front
of any altar you wish—there are many along the sides and
also small chapels jutting off here and there. The sponsor of
the "Firenze Maggio," the Princess of Piedmont, attended
this performance, as did also the Prince and Princess of
Jugo-Slavia who were visiting here. We, of course, had to
await their arrival before the concert began and they came
about a quarter to ten! At the end we again had to wait before
leaving—until they left—the doors simply not being opened.
So we got out around midnight. All streets were closed to
traffic and we couldn't get a tram home so had to walk. But
I was glad because we again saw all the soldiers lined up on
both sides of the street all the way to the station, where we
had to pass, and then we saw several different companies in
the most fantastic costumes, and the band, and what not.
I guess the Jugo-Slavic royalty left on that night train. My,
how these people do love the pomp and circumstance! The
officers with the egret feathers in their helmets struck Mrs. W.
awfully funny and she'd pull me back, boldly point to them,
and laugh uproariously. I was scared stiff we'd be called on
it. She has so many of these foreign mannerisms, queer little
childish naivete—getting a lot of amusement out of some
little thing that bores me to death.

Monday night I went to see "William Tell" (Guglialmo
Tell), . . . The ballet in it was positively the loveliest I've
ever seen anywhere. The costuming and scenery also were
topnotch. The singers were not as good as those in "Il
Trovatore."

Just as Clara had opinions about political situations, she also had them about music and art, as evidenced in the next few passages. Clara noted that Ascension Day is a national holiday in the Catholic country of Italy. The custom, she explained, is to buy crickets in tiny cages and take them to the church to be blessed in order to bring luck during the year. The letter also describes a variety of excursions she'd undertaken earlier in the month.

Florence, Italy
May 18, 1939 (Ascension Day)
I went to Bach's St. Matthew's Passion at the Teatro Communale. The music was grand—must have been—Bach didn't write any other kind. But I guess one has to "know" his compositions before one can thoroughly enjoy them, and maybe the crickets and Fiesole had made me too tired. One of the Swiss girls here says that when she goes to hear Bach she is sure to see to it that her day is a quiet one so that her mind is not tired in the evening. But anyway, I'm glad I went. After all, one can't learn the finest music by never hearing it. Next time it may mean more to me. The choruses were beautiful, especially, "O Haupt voll Blut und Wunden."

Another thing—I know I don't care about German singers. They put on too much. I've heard "The Flying Dutchman" by Germans. There is such a great difference. And when I think back to "Aida," which I saw in Chicago, I can't help but like our American and "Americanized" artists the best of all! They seem to take it so much easier, both singing and acting. The Italian and German opera principals that I've seen these past two weeks, and especially the German, have me quite physically tired by the end of the performance. (I don't say "evening" because they end all the way from midnight to 1:30.) Their jerky walking, as tho their shoes were filled with lead, their arms upstretched or outstretched

99% of the time in the most exaggerated fashion—well, they
make these vaudeville imitators of operatic stars look mild.
I thought that sort of thing had gone out with the fat prima
donnas. But not here. "The Flying Dutchman" last night—the
acting and gestures—amused me no end. (I had the German
libretto with me.)

At eight o'clock in the morning on Tuesday, May 9, we
started out for Lake Como, about 1½ hour ride on the train.
That was "Imperial Conquest Day," commemorating the
conquest of Abyssinia,[2] and special rates on trains were to
be had.

The Lake Como district is as beautiful country as I've
seen anywhere. The high hills were the greenest green;
flowers were everywhere; and over and above and beyond it
all could be seen the white snow caps of the Italian Alps. It
was marvelous!

There is another exhibit here centering around the
Medicis—in their palace. I am still deep in the study of their
history and this exhibit is therefore extremely interesting.
I went again the other day to see some of the things with
a "closer glance." Some of these illustrated books of real
parchment have me all excited. The other day I had a
pencil with me and began to copy—sketch some of the
little cherubs floating along the edges of the books. It was
quite fun, and the darling infants really did look like what I
wanted them to look like—only with the bulges in the wrong
places—like looking into one of these "screwy" mirrors at
carnivals.

There were a number of music books—one took my
fancy especially—dark or bright blue background with gold
notes; on the opposite page, deep red background with gold

---

2. Ethiopia.

notes—queer square- or diamond-shaped notes. Saw some original sketches of Michelangelo's.

Last Monday evening I attended the Monte Carlo Ballet, and if ever I was thrilled, it was that evening! One of the numbers was the "Blue Danube." Imagine, if you can, a combination of toe-dancing, aesthetic, adagio, and just plain graceful waltzing thrown in here and there, and you have what I saw. One girl had on a short brown velvet dress and had row upon row of narrow white lace ruffling as a lining of the skirt; and also had short panties made of the same ruffling. Of course, she had that skirt up in the air most of the time, and these lace ruffles looked lovely! She was supposed to be a flirt trying to cut out another girl (the star of the evening), and she did the flirting stunt exceptionally well; it showed in every move she made. She was the only performer who received flowers outside of the star.

There is an exhibit in Florence of industrial arts, and I visited one this afternoon. How I wish you had been with me instead of Mrs. Wasilko. Her tastes and mine are extremely different, and the exhibit at which I wanted to gaze an hour she'd hurry by or criticize. She was especially hard on the glass, remarking that the only true art in glass is in Norway or Sweden. She was bemoaning the fact that these Italians didn't stick to their ancient art in glass rather than try copying modern things. (This silly idea of trying to keep Europe medieval—or this part of it anyway. The fact that perhaps the ancient art is no longer demanded in the market of today, and that these people must go modern in order to make a living wouldn't occur to her at all. That would be sacrificing art to gross lucre. What the poor people might be eating is another matter that wouldn't occur to her either—and to many like her. Of course, I didn't say that to her, or I would have been in for at least an hour of dissertation, getting nowhere.)

It was not like Clara to hold her tongue. Her appetite for a good argument may have started in high school, when, as a member of the Lincoln Debating Club in 1912, Clara argued the affirmative on the question of women's suffrage.[3] Years later, she took pleasure in describing an argument in which she prevailed. According to an item in the *Wausau Daily Record-Herald*, Clara's presentation to the Wausau Lion's Club upon her return in 1939 included a reference to British people she encountered on her "globe-girdling adventure" who considered American World War I soldiers "worthless," claiming that the United States entered the war only "when the allies had it nearly won."[4] Clara no doubt held her head high when, according to the article, she declared that her "conclusive refutations of these charges left these British with no reply."

Clara's delight in animated discussion is also apparent in a letter written in June but that refers to diary entries she made while in Florence. (How I wish her diary had survived!)

The man had been in the Ethiopian war. I asked him the whyfor of it all. One argument was that after Italy had a great empire she would no longer have to worry about trade. We touched the question of over-population and here he was awfully funny. With just the hint of a twinkle in his eye, he said Italians had too many children, but (and he became serious again) he justified it because he said at the rate Italy was going, she would in a few years have enough of a population to man a huge army and navy, whereas France, at the rate it is going in race production, will soon have

---

3. "High School Notes," *Wausau Daily Record-Herald*, March 18, 1912.
4. "Miss Clara Pagel Gives Sidelights on News to Lions; Wausau Traveler Tells of Observations in Trip around World," *Wausau Daily Record-Herald*, October 31, 1939.

no population at all with which to maintain an army, and therefore Italy can get what it wants by intimidating the other nation—won't even have to resort to actual war!

He complained that out of the World War, Italy got no colonies, where France and England got plenty. He did not want to believe me when I said America got no territory and that we wanted no colonies. My, but he was an interesting person—intelligent, and with enough fire to make the argument pretty lively in spots.

The following day I had another interesting conversation with my teacher.[5] . . . We also spoke about war. I'd rather not write about that; one can never tell when these letters may be censored. She told a beautiful story about Mussolini, but it would take too long to repeat. I have it in my diary and some day you and I will have a diary-party.

Clara's mother had come from Germany, as had her father, so Clara had some facility with the German language and frequently put it to use in order to stimulate conversation. In a further attempt to mitigate language barriers, Clara went beyond using a phrase book to taking private Italian lessons while she was in Florence. Here is another diary entry relayed in a letter in which it's clear that Clara could establish good will even without a common language. Her irrepressible curiosity and her desire to peer deeper into the world are also evident in this passage.

One afternoon I went to one of the palaces with the mother of the German girl at the house. The guide spoke English and French. She understood a little French and what she couldn't get, he'd tell me in English and I'd translate in <u>my</u> German. It really was a scream—and the guide was somewhat of a clown

---

5. Clara's Italian teacher, Miss Campana.

and by the end of the afternoon we were almost hilarious. It pays to try to get—well, shall I say "on the good side of the guide"—because he has keys to everything, and he can open more doors and chests and closets and secret passages.

Clara practiced speaking Italian with a man whom she initially referred to as Mr. Celli but later called Enzo, as he more frequently accompanied her on excursions. As Clara reported in a May 3 letter, "Oh, my Italian is coming along fast. The baggage carrier is 'fachino' (fah-keeno), not 'pakeeto' as I said. Mr. Celli corrected me, but he said, with a twinkle in his eye, 'You know we Italians are so clever, we know what you Americans mean, no matter how you speak the Italian.' " Mr. Celli seemed quite charmed by Clara.

Wherever Clara traveled, she observed how women lived. In some ways, Clara could relate to Miss Campana, her language teacher. Like Clara, she was unmarried and had spent years caring for her mother. When Clara described Miss Campana's life as "cramped," I believe she was also describing her own life before the YWCA opened its doors in Wausau.

I had my lessons from eleven to twelve, and luncheon at one o'clock, so I went over to sit in the large park to read for that hour. Miss Campana seemed rather worried about that and warned me to be very careful for fear somebody would come up and annoy me. She said, "Do not go far into the park, Signorina, and if you wish to sit down, sit on a bench where someone else is already sitting. If you sit on a bench all alone, some person is very likely to come over and annoy you." This was broad daylight—noon—when there are hundreds of people coming from work and passing along that way! It gives you an idea of how shut-in Italian women are. It isn't so bad now, according to my observation of things in general, but it must have been awful in the old days. Miss Campana is a little older than I am and I have a hunch has led a very cramped life between her mother and church work and charities.

In her effort to deepen her experience of the world, Clara was open to all excursions, even those for which she might initially have little enthusiasm. In her description of a walled Italian garden, for instance, we see an indication of how she experienced life, especially in this line: "You walk way down this path and get all excited, and suddenly, while stopping to admire a particularly lovely rose specimen, you happen to glance back the way you came and see another path leading over in the other direction that looks even more enticing than the one you are on." She was intent to see behind the wall of this Italian garden, just as she was intent to see behind the "wall" of a person, a culture, and even life itself. The freedom to explore where her curiosity led was exhilarating for her.

Florence, Italy
Sunday, May 28, 1939
I have just returned from a trip to an Italian garden, and I'm still holding my breath. One of the Swiss schoolgirls and I started out for a little village up on one of the high hills around Florence, called Fiesole (Fee-ay-zoh-lay—in Italian one pronounces every letter and every vowel), and when we went down the street we noticed that there were dark clouds in that direction. Thinking it might be raining up there, we started out in another direction without any set destination. We crossed the Arno River and this girl (the girls call her "Trude"—I don't know her last name) suddenly asked if I would care to go up on a hill just a short distance beyond the river to get a fine view of the city from there. Well, I don't care much about these fine views from some hilltop; they never did appeal to me; but, of course, in these countries you are so

likely to run on to something so interesting along the way that
I never refuse when anybody who knows the lay of the land
asks me to go along. The more country I traverse, the more I
become acclimated and the more I feel at home.

This proved no exception. We walked to the top of
the hill thru—well I won't say lane—rather we walked
up an extremely steep hill along a stone-paved "via," very
narrow, between stone walls all the way from about five
feet to perhaps 12 feet high. Every little ways there would
be another little "alley-way" (and yet the word "alley" does
not sound right) branching off to the right or left, or we
would run up against some very old "villa" which we could
tell, by its architecture or the way the walls were built, to
be some 400 or 500 years old—and then I'd get all excited
about the inevitable wrought-iron lamp on the corner or the
iron-barred windows, or the heavy wooden doorway, etc.
Finally we reached the top, pretty tired out with the steep
climb to say nothing of having tired feet because of the stone
pavement. We ended right up against a doorway in a stone
wall at least fifteen feet high, over which we could see trees
and the tops of life-size statues. Trude said it was a private
villa garden and that we might visit it at the cost of two lire
(10 cents). There seemed to be nobody around, but we did
see a bit of wire with a handle at the end—which we thought
looked as tho it might be pulled—and we pulled it. Suddenly
the door sprang open and we stepped inside. And what an
inside!

To hide the wall from the inside were hedges, cut just like
the stone wall itself, i.e., about a foot or two wide by some
10–15' high. It presented a solid mass of thick green—looked
to me like a sort of myrtle. On every side were roses. I have
never seen roses like there are in this city. Some are actually as
large as the largest peonies. Here there were all kinds and all

colors—the loveliest shaped wild roses, some others of a red so deep that the velvet "sheen" of it was actually black. There were long borders of them—yellow, red, pink; bushes, trees, vines. The garden is huge, on the side of the hill (the opposite side to that which we climbed), and terraced. The paths are all lined with low box hedges, perfectly clipped. There is a water-lily pond with the loveliest large pink and white flowers, and, of course, being in Italy, the inevitable fountain-statue in the middle. This part of the place brought forth my greatest enthusiasm.

We were at the lowest part of the garden, and I happened to glance up. I could hardly believe my eyes! I know I've seen pictures of these gorgeous Italian gardens, but I always thought the artist took an "artist's liberty," but now I know he didn't even do his subject justice. Imagine being surrounded by roses, the air filled with their fragrance. Just in front of you the lily pond; then a short space of lawn; beyond that some more roses, and a few "trimmed" trees (formal designs, but graceful ones)—and just beyond that the tall, tall hedge that hides the outside wall, with a number of these very tall thin cypress trees (like our Lombardy poplars, but much "thinner" and deeper green), with the row of statues, a sort of greying white against the final extremely tall trees growing around the place—like our maples and pines. I shall never forget the sight.

Clara had long dreamed of a trip around the world—one that went deeper than a tourist's experience. She wanted to awaken new and more fully informed perspectives. She wanted to feed her spirit, challenge assumptions, open her eyes. While living her dream, she was truly awake—awake to world events, awake to her prejudices, awake to magnificence in the unfamiliar. As the letter continues, we can see the impact the trip is having on her:

At first I was quite disgusted with these age-old stone villas—
which is the drawback when one stays but a few days in any
place. It is so easy now for me to understand how one writer
can come away from Florence and disgustedly write about
these ugly square stone buildings romantically called "villas"
that are without any kind of decent heat; about climbing a
hill and reaching the top absolutely out of breath and with
throbbing feet; and entering churches that are so dim you
can't see a thing, and which are so cold you freeze nearly to
death; and eating your meals with sweaters and coats on; and
doing without good butter, good coffee (or any coffee at all),
good milk—being content with breakfasts that consist of
only cocoa and rolls—absolutely nothing else, in this house,
and in many hotels even—and a lot of other inconveniences.

But I can also—am now beginning to realize after some
three weeks here—understand how another writer can
rave about the churches, the villas, the palazzos (pah-lahtz-
ohs), yes, and even the darned old stone pavements—and
forget all the little inconveniences. After all, one must have
something to complain about or to criticize these European
cities for. I was told at the beginning that I would become
attached to Florence, and it is proving true. I am going to
leave reluctantly. The Italians may be poor—that is, the great
working class—but it is not noticeable. They impress me, on
the whole, as being happy. One noticeable trait is their deep
love for their children—and there are children everywhere!
There seems to be so much more family life here. Of course,
only the well-to-do have cars; there aren't many cars around
here in Florence; but everybody is out in the open air—
strolling along with their children and their babies. Time and
again I have noticed how a loving pride shows in the very
bearing of a father as he strolls along with his little son. There

is also this sort of loving devotion noticeable in the wife toward her husband—the children for the mother.

Perhaps I sound sort of sentimental in that paragraph. The above is merely an idea of the general impression I have been getting from casual observation. I am so glad that the fates decreed that I spend a little part of my life among the Italians. They are no longer "dagos"[6] to me—fruit vendors, ditch-diggers, organ-grinders, gangsters, anarchists or even the disgusting Abyssinia grabbers. They are very nice people, who, I think, are quite puzzled about all this so-called war business and even indifferent about it. They are kind (and I now speak from a tourist's point of view) and do not laugh or stare when a foreigner stands in the middle of a street with a guidebook in hand, looking at a building or even when that foreigner enters their churches and walks up to their altar steps and in front of their sacred images and even behind their altars to view the paintings.

By this point in her journey, Clara seems to have shifted her perspective about what she has frequently referred to as a "lack of respect" for women. The letter continues,

> . . . If I were to talk of chivalry, for instance, I'd keep my mouth tightly closed. Chivalry may have come from this continent of knighthood, but I'd say it had migrated to the grand old USA during the 19th century when so much of Europe that was fine migrated there. (I'm thinking about our own ancestors in that sentence!) . . . I really won't know how to act when

---

6. Per the *Oxford English Dictionary*: "A name originally given in the south-western section of the United States to a man of Spanish parentage; now extended to include Spanish, Portuguese, and Italian people in general, or as a disparaging term for any foreigner."

I return home. I am at the stage now where I simply don't
expect any man to show me any deference. I almost fell over
last Sunday when a man got up in a crowded bus and offered
Mrs. Wasilko a seat. She says it has happened before and
she thinks the man thinks she is lame. So she always carries
a cane. It isn't impoliteness on their part; that sort of thing
just isn't done here. If the sidewalk is only two feet wide (and
many are) and you meet a man, he doesn't expect to step
off for you; he may and he may not. You sort of gauge your
action according to his; if he seems to be edging to the off
side, you press against the wall and pass; if not, you merely
step off, and that's all there is to it. You get to the point where
you just can't be bothered about all these little things. When
I get home I'll expect a man to take off his hat when I enter
an elevator, and if he doesn't, I'll get quite excited about it,
relate the incident to this one and that one for several days
thereafter, and feel quite insulted for days—perhaps even
give the man the dirtiest look I can contrive to manage.
Incidentally, my disposition (which is horrid to begin with)
is getting even more storm tossed. Here I don't expect it at
all; the hat doesn't come off, and in two minutes I even forget
that I had ever seen a man in an elevator. So what?

Clara continues with more descriptions of sightseeing and
her reaction to what she is learning. Her excursions sometimes
cause her to lament her lack of knowledge, reinforcing why this
journey is important to her.

I went to one museum in Florence that made me feel as
though I had been transported bodily back to the 15th
century. I could almost see the men in armour and the
ladies in their exceedingly heavy robes; I could almost hear
the groans of the men who were being tortured in the large

prison downstairs—and these people did indeed have the torture business down to fine points. I don't understand how human beings could possibly think of such terrible things....

Visited a monastery outside of Florence—one of the most interesting places I've ever been. It is on top of a small steep hill. There are supposed to be monks (Carthusian) living there in individual cells who never speak except on Sundays. I do not think the organization is as strict or severe now as it was originally. The old monk who took us around was a most jovial old soul with a ringing laugh just ready all the time. One person asked him if the monks never left the monastery. He said he couldn't answer that question because it was a sin to tell a lie! Wish I could have understood enuf Italian to have gotten into a discussion with him on his idea of life in general. They made wines at this place—chartreuse, I believe it is called. It is a shame that I don't know anything about wines; this is the country where the best is to be had. In fact, it's a shame that I don't know a lot about a whole lot of things.

This German woman and I went to Pisa together—only about two hours from Florence. It was a gorgeous day. The only thing really to see there is the leaning tower and the Cathedral, the Bapistry and the "Campo Santo"—a burial place extremely unique. These are all grouped together at one side of the city.

I was terribly surprised at the tower. It leans much more than I thought possible; and it is much larger in diameter and much less in height than I had imagined from pictures. I often wondered what the tower was for in the first place. It is the "campanile" of the cathedral. Nearly all churches in Italy have these "campaniles" (rather "campili" for plural—cam-pan-eel-ee), which are nothing more than the bell towers. Why they put them separately I do not know. I personally do not like them; they tower far above the church, and in architecture or design seem to have no connection. We walked to the top of the tower, but I am no longer enjoying those heights. Since I hurt my ankle in Shanghai I seem to have developed that same queer fear of height and especially of any buildings of stone. The "Bapistry" is usually a small round building in which babies are baptized—used only for that purpose. (At the rate babies come into this country I think it is quite a necessary necessity.)

Even as Clara engaged in sightseeing and soaking up the culture, she confronted perspectives that challenged her own. She longed for frank discussions about international politics and its impact on ordinary people, but Italy in 1939 was neither the place nor the time for that. In a May 28 letter, she mentions attending a concert with a Dutch woman she met in the pensione who had traveled a great deal and spoke English very well. Clara reports, "Her views are surprisingly American, and we exchanged ideas about Italy. It was rather a relief to exchange views with somebody who wasn't so pro-Italy and pro-European that they couldn't brook some genuine criticism and discussion." Although Clara's letters provide some information about her perspective on the government in Italy, there's certainly a lot she doesn't say.

Clara's understanding of what was occurring during this lead-up to World War II was based primarily on conversations— which is not to say that she believed everything she heard. She recounts a conversation with Signora Bianca de Filla, owner of the pensione in Florence where she was staying, who believed that "China will be better off when Japan takes it over." Clara's ability to think for herself is evident in her reaction to the signora's opinion: "It shows that the Rome-Berlin-Tokyo propaganda has made its impression all right. The signora claims she knows it's

true because she has 'heard it said.' Just as credulous as can be! If
everything were true because we have heard it said—whoopee."

Florence, Italy
June 1, 1939
War: I've had so many interesting comments the past few
days. There is one young German girl here attending the
University, and her mother came to visit her for a few days.

She says Hitler cannot start a war—Germany simply
cannot afford one. Wish you could listen in on the
conversations we have. I hesitate to put things into letters.
After all, I am a guest in a country of strict censorship, and
as a guest I feel I must respect its wishes. You can see even
I am beginning to annex a little of this queer fear of saying
something that might put the other fellow in bad with
either the German or the Italian government. It's in the air.
A German "Geschaeftsmann"[7] and his daughter came here
yesterday and he and I had a grand long discussion this
morning at breakfast. He is clever. We talked a long time
and he never said one thing in criticism of Hitler or the
government. He admitted that the German is afraid to talk,
but he says one gets accustomed to speaking of other things.
Wise man. He is well along in years and speaks Italian and
English very well.

Anyway, I have no fear of war in Europe. I haven't seen an
American newspaper since, I believe, Colombo—or was it
Manila. I've seen a New York *Herald-Tribune* here, published
in Paris, but it contains mostly gossip of Americans in Europe.
So what is going on in the world I know not.

---

7. Businessman.

In June, Clara rather suddenly felt she'd had enough of Florence and decided to go to Genoa. On the way, she stopped in Milan to see the da Vinci exhibit but got stalled there by what she refers to as "red tape" related to shipping packages home. In this letter to Irma, Clara explains her frustration:

Milan, Italy

June 13, 1939

I have mailed packages from all over, as you know, and never have I had this difficulty. I get all kinds of explanations—Italy doesn't want any money to get out of the country (I think by this they mean money in the form of merchandise); America doesn't like Italy and vice versa (altho I think this is bunk). The best reason was the bellhop's this morning, who says that since no country nowadays wants to buy from any other country, Italy is keeping its exports and imports in perfect balance. They register every single package that is sent out and every pound that comes in. No doubt this is the real idea back of all the red tape. This country is so bound by rules and regulations that I think it has become mummified in the process—and if you remember how the mummies in the Field Museum are bound up round and round and round from head to foot, you'll get my idea. I honestly believe the people are happy and content with it all.

Aw, I'm in a blue mood today—not bad, but so-so. In front of me is one bag open, disclosing a lovely Greek vase with its graceful handle broken off and in two pieces. I have a touch of athlete's foot between my two little toes on the left foot and by the throb I fear there is some infection; the poor little toe is almost raw on the inside, although it worries me more than it hurts. Since the awful ankle episode of China days, I pay more attention to little things like this.

And I'm wishing more than ever that you were with me.

Yesterday morning at breakfast I kept "talking to you" in my mind, thinking how you would laugh at the rolls-and-coffee breakfast, and how we'd plan to spend the rest of the lovely sunshiny day, and how we'd plan on where to go next after Italy—oh, and just the grand, super-grand relief of having you with me, knowing that every word I'd say would be understood and that I would understand everything you'd say—in other words, there'd be an anchor for me.

Clara continues disclosing her insecurities and homesickness to Irma as she describes a man she encountered the previous evening:

Last evening at dinner, I noticed a young man sitting at the next table. He looked <u>so</u> self-conscious and ill at ease, and I was feeling sorry for him, knowing just how he felt. (I've had my share of that sort of thing off and on.) I was wondering whether he was an American or German (something I seldom have to wonder about as the Germans are so terribly evidently German and no mistake!). I was sure he was American except that he just didn't have that confident air, and what's more, he was wearing a button on his coat lapel. These Germans and Italians all wear some kind of button, and sometimes two or three or more. But I soon forgot all about him in roaming around in my own mind like quicksilver. Suddenly I came back to earth by a voice inquiring, "Would you mind if I'd sit down and talk to you a while?" I almost jumped! Then I was sure he was an American—and a very lonesome one. But he was Canadian—born just across the lake from Upper Michigan—so he wasn't so very far from being an American. Seemingly he is a college pedagogue and is studying or rather looking at the art of Italy and France and Spain (the Spanish Art Exhibit being in Genoa just now).

He asked if I were traveling alone and was dumbfounded —simply aghast—to think I was not only traveling alone, but that I had no family in the world. By the way, he said, "Oh, I think that's terrible; that's just simply awful!" You'd think I must be the most miserable human being on earth. He thinks Milan is the most repulsive city he's ever been in. (And I think it is the best I've been in in Italy; I like the place!) Every word; every act showed his homesickness and loneliness. I was, I guess, just as sorry for him as he was for me! It's very seldom that I don't much enjoy a conversation with anybody who happens to come along, but I was surprised to find myself slightly bored with him. He was so definitely in the dumps that it began to wear on me and it made his conversation boresome—almost—and it could have been just the opposite because he knew volumes about art.

Clara seems intrigued by the perspective of a tour guide who explained why democracy would not work in Italy. His words in the following excerpt remind us that there were times when the United States was not perilously polarized:

Milan, Italy
June 13, 1939
I was so amused at a remark of a guide at the da Vinci exhibit yesterday. We had been deep in discussion thru two or three galleries, and finally sat down and went on for fully a half hour. He said there was this difference between Americans and Italians: two Americans could argue about the political situation of their country and still be friends; two Italians would end up in one awful fight. He added that this is why it is really necessary that one man be at the head of this country, and not a "government by the people."

Clara arrived in Genoa on June 14. She says she would have loved to stay in Genoa for more than one day "to find out just where all these streets lead to," but we sense that she is preparing to move on from Italy.

Genoa, Italy
June 15, 1939
This is the most amazing city! I think it is almost as
fascinating and unusual as Venice. It seems to be built, not
on hills (like Cincinnati!!!), but on cliffs and precipices.
There are a number of funicular rails scattered about the city,
and one can take <u>elevators</u> from one street up to the next!
The place seems filled with long, long tunnels, too—in fact
this is a city of a number of stories—Empire State Building
expressed in a city. I've never seen anything like it.

Part of Clara's appeal is that she did not take herself too seriously and she enjoyed bantering. Several examples are included as the letter continues:

I wish I could take life easier—fall in with the routine and
not constantly be doing differently and constantly analyzing
<u>why</u> I insist on being different and then wondering why I
can't be like other people—if you get what I mean. I sincerely
trust you are deeply engrossed in my personal problems, so
that you are breathlessly reading this paragraph to its bitter
end. Never mind, if I get much more analytic or much more
different, I'll chuck it all and come home . . .
     By the way, I was teasing an Italian the other day about
Al Capone and a few other of the gangster type that represent
this country in America, and asked him not to send over any
more of that sort. At the same time, of course, I said I was well

aware that we had another kind of Italian—Caruso, Muzio, Gigli—but that naturally not everybody knew these as well as they did Capone. Then this fellow said, "What about Columbus?" Well, you know, I'm quite ashamed of myself, but it didn't dawn on me until then that Columbus <u>was</u> a Genoese! I was so taken off my feet that I simply had to admit my momentary ignorance; he could see that I was surprised. Columbus and Spain are so closely linked in my mind—I think more so right now as I heard a lecture on stamps in which the lecturer pointed out the number of Spanish stamps that commemorate things about Columbus. Anyway, here I am in his home town and I believe will be seeing a Columbus Museum this afternoon.

Late afternoon
Just returned from the afternoon tour of the city. . . . When the guide learned I was American, he insisted on sitting with me and talking and talking, telling me all his family history—and ending up, as so many have done these past few months, by boldly inquiring why I have never been married—a young lady as beautiful and intelligent as I am!! Some day I'm going to sock somebody! These people of Asia and Europe simply cannot understand why any woman should be single; it just isn't in their code. The way this afternoon's guide ranted along you'd think I was Columbus himself—so brave was I to be traveling all over the world alone—to be even going out into the city of Genoa this morning and, think of it, going up on a funicular railway and exploring various parts of the city—all alone! He was dumbfounded. . . . Finally, he suggested that I hire a companion to travel with me. (Again this theme song of being a very rich person.)

Clara found this guide uncharacteristically outspoken on political matters.

The guide today, surprisingly, said, "But we are <u>not</u> all satisfied in Italy with our government." I told him that very few Italians said that, and he admitted that, because he was very old, he was fearless in his comments. In fact, he said more alarming things than anybody else has said to me, and for a few minutes I wondered whether it wouldn't be better that I take a train out tonight!

By this point, Clara was wrestling with where to go next:

I guess it is about time I cut out all this silliness and just hop a boat to South Africa and over to South America and be done with it. Europe has lost its appeal for me, now that you cannot come over. It's like having a grand luncheon served and inviting your best pal, and then the pal can't come—and altho the food is the best, and the music is the best, and the service and atmosphere is perfect in every respect, yet, since the salt hath lost its flavor, wherewithal can it be salted? Again demonstrating that happiness is all in the mind. I read a sentence last night that hit me squarely between the eyes: A fellow who traveled a great deal wondered why people ever traveled at all; didn't they know that real happiness was in their own minds, no matter where they were?

Altho, really, I'm not traveling for happiness, exactly. Right now I'm traveling to increase my woefully limited fund of knowledge—and the more I travel the more I realize how much less is the knowledge gained in books than that gained by living, if only for a short time, in another country.

I did some inquiring about the boat trip around Africa and it sounds orful exciting. I sometimes fear that by now you are thinking I've gone entirely nuts, and I also fear that you are quite right. The wanderlust has a stranglehold on me, but it's for the sea (even if I am the poorest sailor in the world) and the far-flung places—not Europe.

Against the backdrop of all she had observed in the preced-
ing weeks, the conversations she had had with individuals from
nations affected by the looming war, and the powerful symbols
displayed in Italy, Clara paused across the street from the American Export Lines office in Genoa to watch a parade of soldiers
returning from Spain. The sight caused her to consider how she
felt about her home country and patriotism.

Genoa, Italy
June 15, 1939
As the soldiers passed, I looked up and saw a large American
flag above the door. The street was filled with the Italian red-
white-green flags, and I couldn't help but notice the contrast.
Ours really looked dull in color beside the bright green and
their rather orangish red. Of course, to me it looked like a
bulwark—deep staunch red, solid blue, altruistic white—
confident, subdued but ready to jump in and help anybody;
while the bright red-white-green was a show of bravado,
gaily floating, radiating color and brightness—hiding—
well, hiding the hideousness of trenches in Spain, death in
Ethiopia, perhaps a sudden war. Aw, I guess I'm all wrapped
up in my own country; I'm afraid I love it so much I just can't
see any of its faults—at least not out here. It seems so far away
and beyond anything I've found outside. (No doubt, that is
what every single person of every single country in the world
thinks—so I'm not so original after all.)

~

Although Clara earlier reported uncertainty about her itinerary,
she finally settled on going around Africa to reach South America.
However, she faced obstacles related to visas, transportation lo-
gistics, and baggage. In the meantime, she moved into a pensione
in Nice.

Nice, France

June 19, 1939

I never had the slightest idea that I'd be hesitating in Nice, and now it looks as though I might stay for some time. I am trying to get a boat to South Africa and I'm having more difficulties than a fly on Tanglefoot.[8]

This pensione used to be a villa owned by a wealthy Austrian. It makes me think I'm living in an old castle or in one of these moving picture settings that are used for pictures of Napoleon's time. Of course, all these carpets and drapes and walls are faded, but it only takes a bit of imagination to touch that up.

There is no beach here along the Mediterranean—only stones. But that doesn't stop the people from going in bathing—thousands of them every day. The atmosphere of France is so different from that of Italy. I felt it right away. As you walk along the promenade, people, of course, look at you, but they don't stare. And of all the informal modes of dress—you can simply get away with murder in this place. Everything seems to be so happy-go-lucky. Girls in shorts everywhere; beach costumes of the most extreme type are worn.

In the pensione, she again had the opportunity to meet people from various places. Clara mentions that there were three casinos in Nice, and she and a Dutch woman she met at the pensione went to one of them, staying out until two in the morning. Clara reports, "You'll notice I say nothing about my winnings at roulette; I have nothing to say!" She did, however, report on a cabaret performer who did imitations, "and his takeoff on Mussolini was too funny for words, but when he did Hitler, I thought I'd roll off my chair. I haven't laughed so hard since I left Manila. He spoke

---

8. Tanglefoot was a brand name for a type of fly paper.

French, and if I could have understood it I'd simply have passed out." She also mentions that she met a family from Manila on their way to Spain, which, she says, "made me homesick all over again." Homesickness had taken on a new meaning for her. Clara's letters now make frequent references to how much she missed Manila and its weather.

June 20, 1939
Nice, France
I'm headed for Africa tomorrow.... The boat leaves Venice on the 23d. So tomorrow I take the train to the border, with all the red tape of customs inspection, which is awful for Italy. Then change to a train for Milan and another change to Venice. I've sent to Marseilles for my two bags and am holding thumbs that they reach here tomorrow. And all along the way from Venice on I shall have to try to get my visa for South Africa.

The boat I shall travel on is a combination freight and passenger boat; I couldn't get a straight freight boat from here going in that direction; it seems the freight boats all travel eastward.

I may take a boat from Capetown straight for Rio de Janeiro. The idea is to do what I wanted to do all along— Capetown to Rio; Rio to Buenos Aires; across to Valparaiso and then from there the quickest way back to you. I am just wondering if it would be possible for you to meet me in Rio???!!

Give South America serious thought, will you? I'll cable as soon as I know definitely.

Oh, the package. The little one is on its way, but the big one necessitates an extra trip to the customs bureau because of the Bali headdress which I listed as of no value. . . . I'll be _so_ relieved because that will give me much space in my overloaded bags. (Lady, if you come to South America—grab only your toothbrush and your vanity case—absolutely nothing else! Boy, what a ball and chain baggage can be!)

When Clara returned to Venice, two months after her first visit, she was taken in by the beauty of the fields she saw from the train:

Venice, Italy
June 23, 1939
Here I am again, but this time the weather is absolutely perfect. On the train this morning I almost wanted to melt into it—perfect spring day with a balmy breeze and the countryside just lovely enuf to make you want to cry with contentment. Crops all over Italy look bumptious. I don't believe I ever mentioned the poppies of Italy—no doubt the "Flanders Field" kind. Some fields are just a red blanket. I passed several fields of ripe grain today in which many red poppies and blue cornflowers (I think) were growing, and against the ripe-grain-yellow, the effect was beautiful beyond words. (I don't suppose the owners of that grain crop see it that way!)

Clara's unassuming charisma, determination, and ability to establish rapport shines through her letters, but we don't necessarily know how others saw her. The following passages, however, illustrate the favorable impression this unforgettably spirited woman made on those she met. The first passage refers to her conversation with the British consul regarding her need to get a visa for South Africa. The second passage is about her return to the Cavaletto Hotel, where she had stayed during her previous visit to Venice.

I tried here to get a South Africa visa and no go. My next
attempt will be Port Said and then Beira. The consul didn't
think I'd experience any trouble, . . . When I told him what
trouble there was about Palestine he said, "But you went,
didn't you?" I replied, "You bet we went!" And he just shook
his head and grinned and said he thot I'd get into S. Africa all
right, too. . . .

As I walked in, one young fellow brightened up and
greeted me as an old friend. The clerk's eyes lit up, too, and he
even escorted me up to my room. The one bellhop grinned
from ear to ear. And when I entered the dining room this
evening the waiters were as sweet as could be.

Before leaving Italy, Clara took in one last exhibit and offered
the following critical assessment:

P.S.—Next noon on St. Mark's Square, doves all around me.
Took time out for the Paola Veronese exhibit this a.m.
The halls were all hung with soft grey velvet, the windows
had cream color material covering them completely to give
a soft light. One room was in palest yellow. These hangings
reached from ceiling to floor; ceilings were white; most of the
lighting indirect. There really weren't so many pictures—but
they hung four to six or so in each large room. I still wish
some great artist could come along and paint these religious
pictures more according to what the original scenes must
have been. I can't get any thrill out of a Madonna dressed in
gorgeous brocaded velvet, being crowned by a high-priestly
looking individual with a highly bejeweled gold crown, while
hefty angels tumble all around the clouds at fantastic angles.

9

At Sea

As Clara boarded an Italian steamship on June 23, 1939, she wrote, "I feel as though I'm embarking on a long journey instead of merely continuing on my way." This was the final leg of a journey during which Clara had grown into herself while the world shifted around her. Her intent was to take the *Rosandra*, a combination freighter and passenger ship, from Venice to Capetown, where she would take a different ship to Rio de Janeiro, Buenos Aires, and finally Valparaiso before heading back to the United States. Months at sea would provide ample time to reflect on what she had learned about the world and her reactions to it—ample time to take a long journey of self-reflection.

Initially, Clara was one of only thirteen passengers aboard the *Rosandra*. Some of the ship's passengers were seeking refuge, whereas others were seeking their fortune. Clara was pursuing a better understanding of the world, and what an opportunity she had aboard this Italian ship with hours to spend in conversation with passengers from Italy, Czechoslovakia, Belgium, Britain, Germany, and Portugal—all headed to Africa. She most closely associated with a young man identified only as Benjamin and a married couple with the last name of Pollack, noting this as the first time she had been with an entirely Jewish group. She would later admit to harboring a prejudice against the Jews, which she hoped to overcome.

Clara opened her first letter from the ship with a description of life at sea:

On the Ionian Sea
Sunday, June 25, 1939
I am sitting on a deck chair on the portside (I hope; I never can remember these ship parts) of the "Rosandra" at exactly 6:25 p.m., with the sun just getting ready to set, and the sea as deep blue and as quiet as can be, although there is a spanking breeze that is going to aggravate me plenty by blowing this paper all over.

All afternoon I have been sitting on the foredeck, first listening to Benjamin reading one of Zane Grey's books to me—so that he may get the practice in English—and then crocheting, and later on reading some of Solomon's wisdom in my little book of Apocrypha. (Ernie gave me that book all of 15 years ago, and I am now beginning to read it! It's extremely interesting.)

Tomorrow we make our first stop—at Messina, Sicily— right where the toe of the "boot" strikes the "football." I have always wanted to get my foot on Sicilian soil, and I'm going to have two chances, because later we stop at Catania, a little further down. Then a long stretch across to Port Said. I have come to the conclusion that the sea is the life for me. I no more than was safely tucked away in my cabin the other day than I began to feel calm and contented. Thus far I have not been too seasick—just a tinge of it once in a while.

Three days later, Clara feels less suited to life at sea and also suffers a bout of loneliness:

Seasick!

In the upper berth of Cabin 2

8:15 p.m.—6/28/39

Did I say something the other day about ship life being the life for me? I take it all back! Late yesterday afternoon, when we left Catania, Sicily, the minute we got out of the breakwaters we got into a strong wind, hitting the boat from the left. The heave and roll wasn't too bad, but it was our first, and although I managed to get a little food down at dinner, I left the table suddenly and dove into my berth. And about midnight the wind died down, so I got up, undressed and bathed, and read "The Rains Came" until two a.m.

This morning I had breakfast and sat out on deck—but not for long. The sea is just a wee bit rough. I got to my cabin—shared my breakfast with the fishes—and I have been in the throes of nausea ever since, except a little time out for tea this p.m. just to keep something in my stomach. When I'm in this state, I am driven to wonder whether it's insanity that makes me buy a steamship ticket, or just dumbness.

I just can't raise my head. I have the pillow propped up high enough so that I can write lying down. I think I'm the only one down, as I hear laughter and stamping feet above me in the music room.

A few minutes ago, my table boy came in with some carnations sent by Benjamin and Mr. and Mrs. Pollack (the latter bought a bouquet for his wife yesterday and these are taken from it). They sent a lovely little card, the envelope properly stamped with the ship's post! I was so pleased that I began to cry and just sobbed. Guess I have been feeling lonelier than I had thought. I very rarely admit my alone-ness, even in my own mind. I don't dare.

Mr. Pollack is Czecho-Slovakian—a Jew. When Hitler

took over the country, Mr. P. asked his firm if he might be transferred. They found a place for him in Nairobi, so he's on his way. He's very young, married two months ago to a pretty Jewess of 18. The firm is paying him about $250 a month, with raises promised. He's evidently a crack salesman—covered Czecho-Slovakia and Hungary—was telling me about all the money he had that was taken by the German authorities—I believe around $6,000.

He tells almost unbelievable things. He had just bought a radio—the authorities wouldn't let him take it out of the country—same with a valuable camera. He said they burned many fine books when the Germans came in—any that in the least way dealt with socialism. He speaks German, and I look forward to long conversations with him.

The three Czech couples keep very much to themselves and are the kind who will greet you "good morning" with a completely sober face and evidently feel that they have done their "duty" for the day; thereafter do not expect even another glance from them, far less a word or smile. The elderly Italian lady—looking very lonesome—I find can speak just a bit of English, and I have talked a little to her. I wish she could speak much. It seems her husband is an engineer in Africa and she has had some rather hair-raising experiences in her life, as when one night she was in the jungle alone except for her "boys" (bearers or servants), and she heard a lion approaching. The "boys" were scared to death and climbed to the roof of the shelter. She took her gun and fired. Luckily the lion was frightened and went away.

Clara spent most of her time with Benjamin, who wanted to practice conversing in English. Rather than view language

differences as barriers, Clara found the challenges they posed
an enhancement to enjoyment—although she admits it was
tiring.

My boon companion happens to be a young German Jew! He
is a most charming young man. He does not wish to be called
German; he said yesterday that his father taught him to call
himself a Jew; that was sufficient. I judge him to be about 20;
I think he has been studying in Italy; is now on his way to join
his parents in Elizabethville, Belgian Congo, where the father
is in the vulcanizing business and they have a farm. I think
he said they left Germany two years ago. I asked if that was
just after the big putsch, and he said he did not understand
anything about a big or first or second or third putsch, that
there were killings right along all the time all over Germany. I
asked if he were not bitter, and he said no, because he has an
ideal—that the Jews would one day have their own country
again. He does not want to see Germany punished, because
the German people are not at fault.

Ben says that Germany is definitely creating the coming
war; that everybody who is observing in Italy can see it; that
the Italians hate the Germans; that Mussolini is a tool in
Hitler's hand; that Hitler sends Germans into Italy to conduct
the propaganda campaign—and that Mussolini is not the
leader of Italy, but that the Fascist leader is. (I asked Ben
that leader's name, and he hesitated to give it to me, because
he said it is dangerous to write a thing like this!! So I said if
he wished it, I would not write it. But do you see how this
hideous—or insidious, rather—fear permeates Italy—even a
university student who may never see the country again but
still fears because he is on an Italian ship. Ho-hum!)

The following quips are relayed by Benjamin. Clara spoke German, and so did Irma, to whom this letter is addressed, so she used the German phrases without translation. Clara describes the first one as "a bit sacrilegious, but rather funny."

Benjamin told me of a Jew who said to the Lord, "Wir waren bisher das auservahlte Volk; nun wahle ein aneres aus."[1]

He also asked me if I knew the meaning of the Hitler salute—the raising of the right hand, palm downward and fingers outstretched. I said, no. He said, saluting, "So oc hist der dreck." [2] And, he added, "Man kann auch sin anderes Wort brauchen." [3]

. . . We are all becoming more acquainted and less formal, although I do feel quite set apart "inside" as I note the difference in the European background and an American. I must be so careful in choice of words. I told Ben I thought he was good-looking. He looked displeased and I asked why. He thought I had meant he looked well or healthy and he wondered if I meant that he had not looked healthy when I first met him.

Time became more fluid on the ship, but world events kept intruding as new passengers came aboard, bringing with them news that was not always reliable or, in the example that follows, was misunderstood because of language differences. Clara had earlier noted that a German news radio broadcast could not be understood because the signals got crossed on the ship: "I simply don't know what is going on in the world, except that the King

---

1. "So far we have been the most chosen people. Now choose another one."
2. "So high is the dirt."
3. "You can also use a different word."

and Queen of Great Britain have been in the USA and Japan has been bombing Chungking."[4] In the absence of hard news, Clara was astute in weighing information picked up during stops at various ports. A young Italian aviator came aboard at Catania. Clara seemed quite taken with him.

"Rosandra"
June 30, 1939
He's an adorable young fellow; usually wears a white suit with the queer jacket of Italy that is a cross between the Russian smock and a Norfolk jacket. Over the upper left pocket he wears the wide-spreading gold "wings" of the aviation corps. Today he is wearing a deep French blue, close-fitting shirt and flannel trousers. I'd like to wrap him up and send him home. I could have wept this afternoon when he said, apropos of something in the conversation, that he expects to die in 1940. Being an aviator, and war being so near, he said with him it means just a—and he gestured a swift dive and crash. He is quite philosophical or resigned about it! I said, "But why?" he looked up a word in the dictionary: "Fatherland."

War rumors do persist in floating around. Perhaps now that I'm out of Italy I will be hearing more of them. This lad said that should war break out, this boat would turn back at Mombasa. I was also told that the Italians have a sand-loaded ship ready to slip down into the Suez Canal to be sunk so as to close up the canal the minute war is declared. Queer world. I asked why the Italians took Abyssinia. He said for a military base; certainly not for colonial expansion because Abyssinia is a desert. So that remark cancels all the highly-impassioned speeches by my Italian friends that Italy took the country in

---

4. Chongqing.

order that her excess population might have a place to live. And so it goes on and on. Does Mussolini himself know why he does what he does—or Hitler?

I wonder how the war is coming in Europe? If anything happens before this boat strikes Capetown, it will, of course, mean my jumping from there to South America, or perhaps even New York. I wouldn't care to be on the Mediterranean if there is war in Europe. No doubt no ship would go there anyway. Mr. Pollack, who I think is an alarmist anyway, and, I fear, somewhat gossipy, came to me the other day with a tale that a petrol tanker—ship carrying oil—had exploded in the Suez Canal just after we had passed. I traced the bit of information to its source and found it was his misunderstanding of what the Italian aviator had said. The latter speaks six words of English; Mr. Pollack understands six words of English, but, alas, they're not the same six words.

Even the jokes, understandably, convey a very dark political outlook. Here is a joke told by the Czechoslovakian Mr. Pollack:

Hitler went to Chamberlain and said, "Germany needs the Saar;[5] it is such a small piece; please let us take it." So Chamberlain agreed. Then Hitler went again and said, "Look at Austria. We need Austria for our trade; after all, it is German, and it will make little difference. Please let us take it." So Chamberlain let him have it. Not long thereafter, Hitler came a third time and said, "Now, over there is Czecho-Slovakia. We need that little strip of land badly. Surely such a small territory means nothing; please let us have it." So Chamberlain let him take C-Slov. In just a very short time,

---

5. Saar, a state in Germany, and Danzig, a city in Poland, were contested territory during World War II.

Hitler again approached Chamberlain. This time, "Please, Mr. Chamberlain, it is quite necessary that Germany have Danzig. It is such a tiny city and should make no difference to anybody else. Please give us Danzig." So Chamberlain let him have it. As he was leaving Mr. Chamberlain's office, Hitler noticed Mr. C's umbrella hanging on a hook, and he said, "Ah, Mr. Chamberlain, that is a very nice umbrella. I should like to have it!" Mr. Chamberlain became quite indignant and said, with great finality, "Indeed you shall <u>not</u> have it; that is my umbrella!"

I am getting into difficulties, and getting a little taste of Mr. Chamberlain's dilemma. Mr. Pollack came to me this morning to tell me that he has several hundred lire that he is most desirous of turning into American dollars. Since I can pay tips on the boat in lire, would I please exchange my dollars with him. Yesterday Benjamin came to me with exactly the same request. This afternoon the Italian aviator came to me offering 22 lire to the dollar if I would exchange. (The going tourist rate is 20; the bank rate is 19.) Now the problem is to keep neutral. And a few remarks have been made that just confirm my idea that a Jew is a Jew the world over, no matter the education, the climate, the country, the time, the circumstance. They are suspicious of every act, every word, every person—and I am interested to know whether it is a "defense mechanism" or just a case of knowing themselves so well and thus suspecting all other peoples of the same cunning.

It is really too bad. Suspicion of another person's intentions is a poison that is deadly; it's the trouble with the world today; it wipes out love, fellowship, like a cobra's venom wipes out corpuscles. One of this Jewish trio said the other day that he dislikes compliments because he has found in his (young) life that the flatterer always has a purpose behind the compliment; he is trying to get something out of you. All of them have been so exceptionally nice to me, and now, like a cloud, comes a fourth person with a tiny, tiny drop of ship's gossip, and immediately fear creeps into my mind— a fear that the cloud may be the forerunner of a deluge that will wipe out the pleasant relationship and destroy again my hope that I may lose the prejudice I have against the Jew.

(Oh, this is all very unimportant; not as serious as would seemingly warrant two paragraphs. I merely note it because I want the impression recorded in this letter-diary. And also, I think these little incidents may be of more interest to you than my description of perhaps Victoria Falls or Venice. When I tell the unimportant things, the little everyday things happening to me, I feel as though I have you with me on the trip. After all, if we <u>were</u> together, we would be discussing the people and our reactions to experiences rather than the big things we have been seeing, wouldn't we?)

I'm trying <u>so</u> hard to calm down and not get all worked up about international politics every time I meet another European. So I was terribly proud of myself yesterday afternoon when Ben and I got deep into the question of whether democracies could weather the storm coming. Have you ever heard of Henry George? Neither have I. But Ben has. Ben has a book of his, written about 1880, and Ben is positive that Henry has the solution to all the economic ills of the world, but the great tragedy is that the world will have none of Henry, because the economists who write today are all in the pay of the financiers and said financiers are death on Henry![6] Ben knows exactly what caused the crash of 1929,

---

6. Henry George's book *Progress and Poverty: An Inquiry into the Cause of Industrial Depressions and of Increase of Want with Increase of Wealth: The Remedy* (San Francisco: W.M. Hinton & Co., 1879) sold millions of copies worldwide.

thanks to Henry; Ben knows exactly the solution to prevent future crashes and crises; and, what's more, it is very simple.

And America is headed for the dumps; our laws are all wrong; Americans are anything but free; the propaganda of the millionaire has each and every one of us bound hand and foot; our individual thinking is governed, nay, directed, by each and every individual banker on Broadway.

Sometimes I feel terribly sorry for us and think I shall begin to learn the swan song—until I remember that they are all clamoring for American dollars; and until I remember with what envy almost every European looks at my passport and remarks how fortunate I am that I am an American. (Rapping on wood.)

∽

Clara marks the third anniversary of her departure from Wausau while on the Red Sea:

On the Red Sea
July 4, 1939
After three years, this is the first Fourth that I am spending absolutely away from any indication that it might be our great day. At Shanghai the first year, there were several things doing—the polo game, the ball game, etc., and we also had a holiday from the office. At Manila, of course, July 4 is July 4. But here it might be almost anything. I want to do something with my flag, but, gosh, Italy ain't exactly chummy about the USA and the captain might shoot me!

∽

Colonization of the African continent, along with other types of exploitation, was viewed a bit differently in 1939 than it is today. Clara met two young trappers aboard the ship, Pierre and Rene, and engaged them in conversation to learn all she could. One of them, a Belgian, spoke English.

His grand uncle was the first white man to go into the Belgian Congo. His father and two uncles also spent their lives in work there. When he wanted to enter the same field, his father told him that first he would have to learn everything he could about it. So he entered the Colonie Congo Belge University (I guess that's the proper name) and, for four years, studied hard—forestry, mining, tropical medicine, zoology, etc. He says he can speak almost all the languages of Africa (no doubt he means the main ones). Talking to him is as exciting as reading a travel book.

Clara asked Rene if he knew of Martin and Osa Johnson, the photographers, explorers, naturalists, and authors in the first half of the twentieth century who provided a photographic record of the Congolese wilderness and popularized camera safaris. She relates his response:

His contempt was almost funny. What he said was typical of people who spend their lives in a country and then see somebody else coming in for a few months or years and going back home to write volumes. He said the Johnsons "used" the natives and the animals. (Remember, he cannot speak the English well and one has to sort of guess what he means by his words; "used" might mean something entirely different to him.) He said, "What do they know about animals? Nothing! What do they know about Africa? Nothing!!" I told him they know one thing: How to make a lot of money out of their venture. He agreed with me but added that he had no use for money made in that way.

He and his companion are now on their way to the

interior for four or five years—prospecting for gold and diamonds. They seem to be under contract for several things—pictures (not an American company), trapping for zoos, circuses and museums, exploring and investigating in the interests of science, some work for the government, and this prospecting work. No doubt there are many other angles. Of course, with so much to learn in that vast continent, and so few people going, they have to use those few to cover all angles. . . .

Oh, but this is the grand, lazy life. All afternoon before me with a book, my crocheting, two interesting companions, and the dolphins and flying fish.

Not content to observe from a distance, Clara went ashore when the opportunity presented itself. On this particular excursion with Pierre and Rene, we see that her shipmates are protective of her:

The Goodship "ROSANDRA," between Djibouti and Aden
Sunday, July 9 or 10, 1939
This has been such an interesting day again. We arrived in Djibouti, French Somaliland, early this morning, and about nine o'clock Pierre and Rene went to the city to buy salt; I went along to see the town and get a shampoo. We had to take a launch for quite a ways because our boat was anchored way out in the harbor. Then we took a taxi into the city.

Since it was Sunday, I didn't know whether I could get a shampoo. However, Rene spied a sign saying "Coiffeur," and we went over. It happened to be a barbershop, one of these places that has the whole front open—a sort of hole in the wall. It didn't look any too clean; pretty hard to keep anything looking clean in these hot places when there's no front to the shop to keep the dust and sand out. Rene asked if they could give me a shampoo, and, after some hesitation, they said they could, so he left me there with strict instructions to pay them ten francs, to come over to a certain "hotel" when through, to keep out of the sun, and not to buy anything—"remember, don't buy anything!"

So I sat me down before a mirror and the man pulled up one of these basins that fit back of you so that you just tilt your head back, and he begins to wash. Up came two little darkies[7]—and oh, so black—one with shampoo soap and the other with a teapot of water. Giving my head a good supply of each, the man began to wash—as though my head were a precious bit of spun glass that could bear no pressure. I gestured that I wanted him to rub hard, and the second time he did do somewhat better. After the second rinse, he took one of the towels that he had put around my shoulders and began to rub the hair vigorously. When that towel was pretty wet, he reached for a second one that was around my shoulders; it dropped on the dirty cement floor. Nothing daunted, he merely picked it up, gave it a shake or two, and proceeded to go on drying my hair with it! Then he handed me a comb and motioned to go ahead. I asked if he wasn't going to dry my hair; he couldn't understand; a customer in the shop spoke a little English and interpreted for me. Unfortunately, says the man, they had no facilities for drying hair—so I had to do the best I could with the wet hair in rolling it up. It felt sticky to my fingers! I'm sure all he did was to soak up the dandruff and distribute it evenly all thru the hair. But anyway, I did try to get it cleaned. The water on the boat is hard and seems to be oily.

---

7. Per the *Oxford English Dictionary*: "'Darkie' was used in the nineteenth and twentieth centuries as a derogatory term for a Black person, especially one from the southern US."

Then I walked over to the hotel—about as ramshackle looking as the movie scenes of our western towns way back in the gold rush days. Many tables were outside on the wide sidewalk as usual—everything looking more or less uninviting because of much dust and general dirt—and flies and flies. I sat there and began writing up my hair-wash episode, just noting it down in shorthand while still fresh in my mind (and I've lost the notes, of course), and as I sat there a number of negroes came up to try to sell me postcards, spearheads, knives, kimonos, pajamas, melons, a chicken. Later, when Pierre and Rene returned, there were more vendors—one had a little square of red cloth in which he had tied up a number of very tiny pearls; another came up with crude brass rings with some sort of agate stone settings. I wanted one of those, and Rene bargained for the one I had in mind and gave it to me. (I am sure it cost all of 6 cents and Rene can't understand why in the world I want a trashy thing like that. But its very crudeness interests me, and I am going to try to have it washed with gold or silver when I return.) He was also fortunate in getting an Abyssinian coin with the head of Menelik on it. (That doesn't mean anything to me right now, but Rene gave me strict instructions to hang onto it as "now it is finish! No more!" So I'll look up Menelik when I get home and hang onto the coin.)[8]

There was one youngster hanging around who had his sarong tucked up in the cutest of fashion. I sketched him and handed him a franc; he was so shy and darling.

This is not the first time Clara has referred to drawing. It is a shame that her sketches, along with photos, her scrapbook, and her diary, have been lost.

---

8. Menelik II was emperor of Ethiopia from 1889 to 1913.

Another new passenger boarded at Dante,[9] which is in Soma-
lia (at the time, Italian Somaliland). The biggest salt factory in the
world was there during the 1930s. Clara soon discovered that the
new passenger spoke English quite well.

Between Mogadicio and Chisimaio[10]
Along the East Coast of Africa
Italian Somaliland
Around the middle of July, 1939
I was amused at the number of British expressions he used.
He is one of the few broad-minded Italians who is not afraid
to express an opinion about the political situation of Italy. He
is employed in the salt business and travels all over the Italian
colonies in Africa—Italian Somaliland, Abyssinia, Eritrea—
and, I believe, into the Sudan. He can tell the most interesting
things because, of course, he comes in contact with all the
tribes in the interior. He says many of the natives use salt
as their money, burying it while we deposit our money in
banks. After all, says he, salt is always salt; it cannot spoil. The
company, he says, pays enormous sums of money out every
year for delivering the salt-freight, in other words. They use
every kind of means and every kind of agency—anybody
going into the interior. Salt takes on a certain dignity out here.
In Djibouti were hills and hills of clear salt drying in the sun
or awaiting bagging; there seemed to be acres and acres of the
stuff and the buildings of the concerns making it.

    Dante exists only because of salt—their only export
being that, and the place itself being nothing but salt-fields,
with a few buildings to house the handful of Europeans
(Italians) necessary to supervise and a few huts for the natives

---

9. Hafun.
10. Now Mogadishu and Kismaayo.

employed in the work. (It also exports an essence—or basis of perfume—obtained, I believe, from some small animal—something on the order of amber gris that comes from the whale. The man couldn't give me the English name; I must look it up when I get home.) But salt is the main thing, and it's the only reason we stopped there.

Besides learning about salt, Clara was fascinated by what the man said about missionaries. Her perspective on missionaries had completely reversed from when she first set off on her trip.

The Italian told me of some Catholic missionaries way over at the edge of the jumping-off place, where he stayed a short time on one of his expeditions, and he said that, although the missionaries may convert some of the natives to Christianity, it would be only a matter of a few years and they would turn Moslem—and the reason struck me very funny—perhaps I can remember his words: "Well, you see, the Moslem religion gives them a few rules how to live, what to eat, and something about keeping clean, just easy things that they can understand. Then, too, there are no Moslem priests around to check up on their behavior. I mean, it's easier for them than Christianity." He says Mohammedanism is making great strides in Africa. Certainly Massaua[11] looked like some town in Turkey; the very buildings shouted Moslem. But this remark that there were no priests to check up on the natives interested me. I've given a good deal of thought to our missionary work since wandering around out here, and frankly, any enthusiasm I ever had for missionary work is dead—medical missions, OK—but the type of person—

---

11. Now more commonly spelled *Massawa*—a port city in Eritrea, on Africa's Red Sea coast. The city reportedly has the oldest mosque in Africa.

aw, skip it; why fill up my diary with a lot of criticism when I
can't do anything about it anyway?

Entertainment onboard included music and dancing. Clara
seemed quite popular, as we see in the following excerpt. However, she took breaks from social activities and conversation, rel-
ishing the time she had to write:

Pierre is sitting at my left doing a beautiful French snore;
Rene is just over a little ways to my right, under the steps
leading to the upper boat deck so as to be out of the wind, his
beret fallen onto the floor, and he in a grand doze. It must be
the clicking of my keys that puts them to sleep—I'd hate to
think it was my company. Anyway, it is after lunch when the
whole boat is always very quiet—my favorite time of the day
when I feel all alone and more ambitious than at any other
time of the day.

I have become a sort o' shining light because I can play
the piano—the only one on board who can—and you know
how I can. I've forgotten the "Meditation," which is always
part of that repertoire of mine; I have lost the last half of
"On Wisconsin" and "Aloha O"—but, fortunately, ah, most
fortunately, I still retain the magic notes of "Florine," and
that seems to captivate the admiration of the Czechs—and
even Rene. Rene used to play, and he can still do a few runs,
but even less than I do—so he sits down beside me and
contradicts or criticizes my every move and tells me how I
ought to play!

I've been having quite a time this afternoon. A young
German came on board (Texaco Oil representative in East
Africa), unusually good-looking and unusually good mixer—
ah, yes, very good mixer. He got things going to a point where

the inertia took charge and it wasn't funny any more—to me, at least. Right after lunch, several of us went up to the recreation room or lounge and started the gramophone going and pretty soon began the Lambeth Walk.[12] Then came the Palais Glide, and a fox trot, and a faster fox trot, and a tango, and, and, and—. Besides, to quench thirst, the fellows began ordering Italian wine—bottle after bottle. I drank two or three glasses of it and began to feel my knees weaken. The boys kept on until dinner—and were they lit! Hilarious to the bursting point. Fortunately, the dinner gong sounded and I excused myself to change dress. I wanted to sink thru the floor in the dining room when the German made much to-do over me as he passed my table—until the steward rescued me and somehow got the boy to his own table. I left the dining room as soon as I could, gave instructions to the steward that, in case of inquiry as to my whereabouts, I could not be located on the ship—and I locked myself into my grand little cabin.

Clara was skeptical of what she calls in this letter "tales," such as one told by a British South African man on board who intended to go on an expedition to the "White City."

----

12. The Lambeth Walk and the Palais Glide are both line dances introduced in the 1937 swing era. According to the Edinburgh University Swing Dance Society, the Lambeth Walk was based on a comedy routine in the 1937 English stage production of *For Me and My Gal*, which ran until the theater in which it was showing was bombed in 1941. It is interesting to note that in 1942, the British director Charles Ridley superimposed a soundtrack of the Lambeth Walk over edited clips of Leni Riefenstahl's film footage of Hitler and his soldiers marching, to make it look as if they were dancing. When he saw it, Goebbels was so angry that he left the room, swearing and kicking over furniture. (See www.swingdoctors .org.uk.)

July 22, 1939

"White City" is a place somewhere in, omigosh, was it
Tanganyika—anyway, near the Zambezi and some other
place (!) which is supposed to be literally strewn with gold—
gold nuggets as big as your fist! It seems that only three white
men have seen the place; one was never heard from again and
the other two, when asked about it, will not tell a thing—
seemingly afraid to. Rene had heard about it, too, and put
in his oars when I questioned about it. Their tales were like
the usual rumors on a thing of this sort: Some whites bribed
a native to take them in; the next morning they found him
hung high in a tree, dead . . . natives won't bring out the gold;
gold is sacred to them . . . the climate at the spot is too bad
for any white man to endure . . . one white man got near the
place and a witch doctor visited him one night at his camp,
and finis.

   Isn't there some sort of tale like this about some place in
South America—on the Orinoco River (or isn't that river in
South America?)—or in the Mato Grosso region down there?
Isn't is queer what a fascination gold has for the genus homo?

Clara goes on to express exasperation with people who travel
and are nonetheless oblivious to geography and culture:

(Speaking about the Orinoco River and its relation to South
America—I overheard an elderly Portuguese passenger
talking to the steward just outside my cabin this evening. The
steward was talking about the price of whiskey in Singapore.
"Singapore, ver dat?" asks the Portuguese. "Singapore—
India," came the answer! And this steward was working on
the line that runs the regular South Asia ports—Bombay,
Colombo, Singapore and ends up at Manila or Shanghai,
I believe. Which again illustrates how many thousands of

people are traveling the world ports year in and year out and
never learn a thing nor care to—whereas other thousands
would give their eye teeth to get a glimpse of those same
ports and they'd make the utmost of their opportunity.
Nature and her relentless averages.)

~

Having traversed the Mediterranean, the Red Sea, the Gulf of
Aden, the Arabian Sea, and the Indian Ocean, Clara was off the
coast of Tanzania on July 22, 1939. Here she wrote the last letter
to find its way into a file folder at the Wausau YWCA. About a
week earlier, Clara had written some lines that reveal her drive
and how she navigated through life.

The shore line is beginning to look a little green, although
the ever-present desert sand is unending. We have been
sailing just about a mile or two off shore for the past several
days. It is so tantalizing; I want to fly over just to have a peep
beyond those hills. I keep wondering and wondering what is
on the other side; sometimes my curiosity settles into almost
physical pain. Are there any animals? Are there any natives?
What kind of vegetation? Why don't we see some kind of life
along the way? (At Dante there is no water; the inhabitants
depend on passing ships for their entire supply! The food
of the natives consists of rice mostly—brought in by Arab
traders in sailboats clear from Bombay! Clever things, these
sailboats; and still more clever navigators these Arabs—using
no compass but the stars, and never deviating from their
course!)

Clara had never deviated from her course, guided by the stars.
Her journey calls to mind words from Tennyson's famous poem
"Ulysses":

Come, my friends,
'Tis not too late to seek a newer world.
Push off, and sitting well in order smite
The sounding furrows; for my purpose holds
To sail beyond the sunset, and the baths
Of all the western stars, until I die.

10

Return

"Miss Clara Pagel Returns from Trip around the World." So reads an almost breathless headline in the *Wausau Daily Record-Herald* on October 19, 1939. The article's opening sentence masterfully sums up Clara's experience, and my guess is that Clara crafted it for the awe-struck reporter: "Keeping just one step ahead of trouble—and usually no more—Miss Clara Pagel returned last night from a three-year trip around the world, traveling by 21 different boats, by train and by air in the three troublesome years since she left Wausau." The next sentence once again shows her dry wit: "Still unable to give any reason for her trip, Miss Pagel resigned her position with the Wisconsin Box Company and on July 5, 1936, left Wausau." I empathize with the reporter, who could not possibly do justice to an exploration of her motivation. Clara no doubt despaired of being able to convey the layers of what she set out to accomplish, so she resorted to self-deprecation.

According to the 1939 article, Clara was able to visit most of the countries bordering the Red Sea and the Indian Ocean because the *Rosandra* made twenty-five stops. She left the boat for a time to go inland to Victoria Falls and Johannesburg, boarding again at Capetown, South Africa. When the ship neared the coast of Nigeria, the captain received a message from the Italian government informing him that war had been declared and that the ship should "lose itself" for a time. They cruised aimlessly for a week before the ship was dispatched to the Cape Verde Islands and then to the Canary Islands, where Clara booked passage on a freighter bound for Rio de Janeiro. Advised by the Argentine and Brazilian consuls that she should not attempt the trip but should return home, she uncharacteristically heeded their warning, but not without grousing that "they did not look with favor on 'a woman traveling alone.' " So rather than going to South America, she transferred to a tiny Italian freighter headed to Montreal.

Clara admitted to the *Record-Herald* reporter that she was seasick 80 percent of the time she was on boats, but she said the final leg of her journey was especially rough because, without cargo, the little boat "bobbed its way across the Atlantic." I imagine that Clara might downplay the entire experience, as she often did in her letters. After describing a harrowing incident, she would sardonically refer to it as just another interesting experience. She was also fond of saying, "All things end. And so did this."

Upon arriving in Montreal on September 28, three months after leaving Genoa, Clara was joined by her friend Irma Gebhard, and the two of them toured the East Coast before returning to Wausau. Once there, Clara went on a speaking tour. Readers of the *Wausau Daily Record-Herald* had followed her exploits the entire time. After the bombing of Shanghai, the newspaper had reported that Irma Gebhard received a cablegram indicating that Clara was safe. The local newspaper also printed two of the letters she'd sent to Irma. Billing her as a "local world traveler" and an "observant world traveler," the paper reported on all of the post-adventure presentations she gave to a range of groups. She told the fifth and sixth graders at John Marshall Elementary School about South Africa and her visit to Victoria Falls and Kruger National Park. She talked to the Irving School's Mothers' Club about children throughout the world and addressed the Missionary Society of St. Stephen's Church and the Lion's Club at the

Hotel Wausau. Clara also addressed the state YWCA conference in Madison, telling of the work of the YWCA in Asia, Egypt, and South Africa. It was reported that she displayed scarves, jewelry, and costumes at the Wausau YWCA's World Fellowship dinner and that she wore an East Indian costume when speaking to various YWCA youth clubs. The saris from India evidently survived her evacuation from Shanghai.

With recent revelations about women's espionage and code-breaking contributions during World War II, I've been asked if Clara might have been a spy. Fifteen hundred women worked internationally for the Office of Strategic Services (OSS, the predecessor to the CIA) during World War II. Could Clara have been a top-secret researcher for the OSS, à la Julia Child, who was posted to Kandy, Sri Lanka? Clara did visit Sri Lanka more than once. She also spent a lot of time in Manila, where Claire Phillips operated a spy ring out of a cabaret frequented by Japanese officers. (Claire's nickname was High Pockets because she smuggled information in her brassiere.) As tempting as it is to put Clara Pagel in a cabaret in Manila, especially because she shared sauciness as well as initials with Claire Phillips, the timing isn't right—Clara had returned home before the United States entered the war and before the OSS was formed in 1942.

Was there another way in which Clara might have worked clandestinely? In 1935, Franklin Roosevelt asked Congress to fund resumption of the diplomatic courier service. Three courier routes were established: the northeast Asia route from Beijing to Shanghai, the southern route from Paris through Rome and Athens to Geneva, and the Iberian route from Paris to Lisbon. Clara's itinerary, curiously circuitous, followed portions of these routes. And she did, after all, work at the embassy in Shanghai. It is romantic to think that Clara might have been a citizen courier, but she could not have been an official diplomatic courier, because no woman held that position until 1972. Whether or not Clara was involved in intrigue, she was an intrepid individual whose exploits included blazing trails and developing relationships.

What Clara chose to do during the short sixteen years that remained of her life following her return is entirely in keeping with the vibrant person I've come to know through her letters. In 1942, at the age of forty-six, she graduated from the University of Chicago with an MBA. She then moved to New York and was employed as a bank analyst by the Federal Reserve.

Clara entered the officer training program at the coast guard academy in New London, Connecticut, in 1943. As Olga Block, Clara's second cousin, once told me, Clara was an "adventurist" and wanted to do something for her country, which had meant so much to her mother. Clara's travel experiences no doubt reinforced that desire, which is perhaps why the Women's Coast Guard Reserve called to her. Referred to as SPARS, an acronym for Semper Paratus—Always Ready, it was formed in 1942. SPARS were the first women to attend a military academy. During the war, the Coast Guard was the only service that trained women officer candidates at its academy.[1] In 1947, having achieved the rank of lieutenant, junior grade, Clara was admitted to the coast guard base in Clearwater, Florida. She also served in New Orleans.

The last several years of Clara's life were spent in the Suwanee Hotel in St. Petersburg, Florida. She had fallen in love with palm trees and balmy weather as she traveled the world, perhaps in part because of poor health. She struggled with weight loss, catarrh, and anemia, and she once was admitted to the Army–Navy Hospital in Hot Springs, Arkansas, for severe rheumatoid arthritis. Clara died in 1955 at the age of fifty-nine. By that time, she had lost her sight—but she had seen the world.

---

1. Robin J. Thomson, "SPARS: The Coast Guard & the Women's Reserve in World War II," USCG, United States Coast Guard Historian's Office, 1922.

It was in 1993, when I attended the first Wausau YWCA-sponsored Women of Vision luncheon, that I learned about the YWCA's mission: to empower women and eliminate racism. Happily employed as the director of continuing education at what was then the two-year campus of the University of Wisconsin in Wausau, I nonetheless was so energized by its mission that I decided on the spot to apply for the YWCA executive director position, which had recently become vacant. On May 21, 2021, twenty-nine years after the launch of the Wausau Woman of Vision award and more than one hundred years after the Wausau YWCA opened its doors, Clara Pagel was honored posthumously as a Woman of Vision. The YWCA empowered Clara to live larger—to travel the world and embrace the unknown with a lively independence. Her story, like the YWCA's mission, continues to inspire me.

Acknowledgments

The shared experience of reading aloud sparked this book's creation. If Clara's letters hadn't been read aloud during meetings of the Blue Triangle Club, they might not have been collected and filed at the YWCA. When I found them, I began reading them to my husband, Lon Newman, who pointed out the significant historic vantage point from which Clara wrote. That started me on a quest to learn about Clara and share her letters with you. Perhaps you, too, will read some of them aloud.

Lon and I had read to one another since the early days of our relationship. When we were both enrolled in a college class on Herman Hesse, I agreed to share the required books with him after he pleaded poverty. It was while I was taking my turn reading aloud a chapter from *Siddhartha* that Lon interrupted to suggest an impromptu road trip. That was in 1972. Fifty years later, we're still taking road trips together.

The pleasure of reading aloud began in my childhood, both at home and in school. My mother, Marion Norgaarden Anderson, and I read all the Little House on the Prairie books—more than once—taking turns reading aloud. It was a cozy activity and no doubt established my love of reading. I attended elementary school in Fountain, Minnesota—a small school with two grades per classroom. The teacher for the fifth and sixth grades read to the combined group after recess. Every year, while reading *Uncle Tom's Cabin*, Mrs. Holsapple would become too emotional to continue so would turn to a sixth grader to read. I was that sixth grader. In high school, I competed in a forensics category called "Extemporaneous Reading," which involved randomly being assigned an excerpt from that year's selected book and, after a few minutes of preparation, orally presenting it. Harper Lee's *To Kill a Mockingbird*, Ray Bradbury's *Dandelion Wine*, and William Saroyan's *The Human Comedy*, three of the books from which I read aloud many times in competition, all had a deep and lasting impact on me.

The joy in reading aloud—and its impact—is being kept alive by the next generation. Books fill the home of our daughter, Rachel, and her husband, Dan Shea. Reading with their boys, Finnegan and Liam, occurs throughout the day—not only at bedtime. During the pandemic, I read to Finn over FaceTime for hours. At age five, he began to read to me. At two, Liam exhibited great storytelling potential through use of dialogue and expression, which he obviously picked up from having books read to him.

The stimulation of reading aloud extends to my participation in The Writers' Circle of St. Croix in the US Virgin Islands. During our Monday morning gatherings, we each read a piece we've written, not to exceed 1,200 words. I found that a weekly goal of 1,200 words was an approach that worked for me in bringing this project to fruition, and this lively group of writers provided me with abundant support and encouragement. Two Circle members in particular, William O'Donnell and the late Bernie Snow, helped me see how I could turn 100 pages of letters into a manuscript. But if not for our leader, Apple Gidley, this book would never have been completed. I was rather new to the island when I contacted Apple after reading her first historical novel. Apple generously agreed to meet with me to hear about Clara, and then she invited me to join the writers' group. Whether I was on or off island, Apple gave me a timely nudge when I least expected it and wise counsel when I sought it. Clara's spirit and story resonated with Apple, and she cares about this project as much as I do.

In addition to family members, teachers, and other writers, those who contributed to development of this book include historians, librarians, booksellers, my publisher, and YWCA colleagues.

Mary Jane Hettinga, former executive director of the Marathon County Historical Society, launched my research by finding Clara's date of death and giving me several leads to people who might have known Clara. Ben Clark, archivist with the Marathon County Historical Society, deciphered references in Clara's letters to places in Wausau circa 1930. Gary Gisselman, now with the historical society and previously a reference librarian at the Marathon County Public Library, assisted me in locating information in both places, many years apart.

Two independent bookstores that are important to me, Undercover Books on St. Croix and Janke Bookstore in Wausau, are owned and operated by determined women. Even though Jane Janke was focused during the pandemic on the survival of the bookstore that has been in her family for more than 100 years, she alerted me to newspapers.com, which became a valuable resource, and suggested that I submit my manuscript to the Wisconsin Historical Society Press.

I appreciate the collaboration with the Press, especially with my editor Rachel Cordasco. Working during the pandemic with three young children at home engaged in remote learning, Rachel helped to restructure the book, which strengthened the narrative. It was serendipitous that Rachel had read the memoir *Shanghai Refuge*, and that she's had a framed copy of Tennyson's *Ulysses* on her desk for a decade.

The YWCA held a special place in Clara's heart, as evidenced not just by her letters and what we found in the archives, but also by the fact that she bequeathed the stocks in her estate to the Wausau YWCA. I am grateful to members of the YWCA Board and YWCA staff during the time of my service as executive director from 1993–1999 and in later years as I began to assemble this book. Former staff member Ellen Hartwig, who searched through the YWCA archives with me in preparation for the seventy-fifth anniversary celebration, shared my excitement when we discovered pictures of Clara. Kathy Garvey, who maintained an interest in the project for more than twenty-five years, contacted me to ensure that any artifacts important to Clara's story would be preserved when preparations were being made to sell the YWCA building. When I needed a safecracker, I turned to Paul Clarke, whose mother was recognized in 1996 as one of the YWCA's Women of Vision. With the cooperation of Andrea Huggenvik, Wausau YWCA executive director at the time, Paul and John Rupple pried open a safe to retrieve Clara-related items.

I was invited by the YWCA's 2021 Women of Vision committee and by Program Director Samantha Wederath to deliver the keynote address for the twenty-eighth Women of Vision event—the first to be virtual. It was also a celebration of the rich history of the Wausau YWCA, which spans more than one hundred years. I was honored to recount Clara's story—and the YWCA's place in it—as she was recognized with a posthumous Woman of Vision award. I was doubly honored when, as a surprise kept strictly under wraps by the committee, I was also named a Woman of Vision. I very much appreciate the touching expression of my connection with Clara and with other Women of Vision who have been recognized since 1993, keeping alive the YWCA's mission to empower women and eliminate racism.

About the Author

Janet Newman began her professional career as a copywriter at a country western radio station and concluded it as a college administrator. In her retirement, Janet participates in four book clubs and a writers' circle. Her writing, which shines a light on fascinating people, has appeared in *Mondays at Ten* and various news publications. Janet and her husband split their time between Wisconsin's Northwoods and St. Croix, US Virgin Islands.